POSH

BY LAURA WADE

★ Revised Edition

★

DRAMATISTS
PLAY SERVICE
INC.

POSH was produced at the Royal Court Theatre's Jerwood Theatre Downstairs in London, England, opening on April 9, 2010. It was directed by Lyndsey Turner; the set and costume designs were by Anthony Ward; the lighting design was by Paule Constable; the sound design was by David McSeveney; and the musical director was James Fortune. The cast was as follows:

GUY BELLINGFIELD	Joshua McGuire
JAMES LEIGHTON-MASTERS	Tom Mison
TOBY MAITLAND	Jolyon Coy
GEORGE BALFOUR	Richard Goulding
ALISTAIR RYLE	Leo Bill
HUGO FRASER-TYRWHITT	David Dawson
HARRY VILLIERS	Harry Hadden-Paton
MILES RICHARDS	James Norton
DIMITRI MITROPOULOS	Henry Lloyd-Hughes
ED MONTGOMERY	Kit Harington
JEREMY	Simon Shepherd
CHRIS	Daniel Ryan
RACHEL	Fiona Button
CHARLIE	Charlotte Lucas

The revised version of POSH received its West End premiere at the Duke of York's Theatre on May 23, 2012. It was directed by Lyndsey Turner; the set and costume designs were by Anthony Ward; the lighting design was by Charles Balfour; the sound design was by David McSeveney; and the musical director was James Fortune. The cast was as follows:

GUY BELLINGFIELD .... Joshua McGuire
JAMES LEIGHTON-MASTERS .... Tom Mison
TOBY MAITLAND .... Jolyon Coy
GEORGE BALFOUR .... Richard Goulding
ALISTAIR RYLE .... Leo Bill
HUGO FRASER-TYRWHITT .... Pip Carter
HARRY VILLIERS .... Max Bennett
MILES RICHARDS .... Edward Killingback
DIMITRI MITROPOULOS .... Henry Lloyd-Hughes
ED MONTGOMERY .... Kit Harington
JEREMY .... Simon Shepherd
CHRIS .... Steffan Rhodri
RACHEL .... Jessica Ransom
CHARLIE .... Charlotte Lucas

CHARACTERS

The Riot Club:

GUY BELLINGFIELD

JAMES LEIGHTON-MASTERS

TOBY MAITLAND

GEORGE BALFOUR

ALISTAIR RYLE

HUGO FRASER-TYRWHITT

HARRY VILLIERS

MILES RICHARDS

DIMITRI MITROPOULOS

ED MONTGOMERY

Plus:

JEREMY, Guy's godfather

CHRIS, landlord of the Bull's Head Inn

RACHEL, Chris' daughter

CHARLIE, an escort

PLACE

A gentlemen's club in London.
The private dining room at the Bull's Head Inn, Oxfordshire.

TIME

The present.

POSH

ACT ONE

Scene 1

A gentlemen's club in London. A wood-panelled room with two big leather armchairs and a small table between them. Jeremy sits in one of the chairs, sipping from a glass of whisky. Guy stands opposite him.

JEREMY. Don't stand there like a schoolboy, Guy — take a seat.

GUY. That a new chap on the desk?

JEREMY. They're all bloody new.

GUY. Told me you were upstairs in the Blue Room.

JEREMY. Idiot.

GUY. I said "Concentrate, mate — I'm not even a member and even I know the Blue Room's the one downstairs — "

JEREMY. Which isn't actually blue.

GUY. Which isn't actually blue. "The one you're talking about, despite having blue walls," I said, "is actually the Oak Room."

JEREMY. Bloody foreign staff. Still, they can book you a cab in seven languages.

GUY. So. How's the mood in the camp?

JEREMY. Oh, you know.

GUY. Amazing, yeah — feet under the table, back in the saddle, ducks in a row, heads above parapets.

JEREMY. Too many metaphors.

GUY. Just the table one, then.

JEREMY. Standing there with a dustpan and brush in your hand, clearing up after someone else's party.

GUY. No, yeah, course. I mean, what, thirteen years on the sidelines? Long winter.

JEREMY. Hard to make people love you when it's all cut cut cut.

GUY. No, sure.

JEREMY. Just set up a group to work on Operation Charm Offensive.

GUY. Excellent.

JEREMY. All they've dreamed up so far is a monthly backbenchers' Curry Night.

GUY. Poppadoms and policy.

JEREMY. Men of the people, you know.

GUY. And women.

JEREMY. People of the people. More offensive than charming, so far. How's college?

GUY. Yeah good good.

JEREMY. Playing any rugger?

GUY. Only when they're desperate.

JEREMY. Your mother tells me you're seeing some girl.

GUY. Well. Yeah. I mean it's not —

JEREMY. Bit out of the loop, aren't I?

GUY. Yeah, it's been a while.

JEREMY. Bit remiss with the godfathering?

GUY. No, god no. I mean I totally know you're here when I need you, so — *(Guy pauses.)*

JEREMY. Drink?

GUY. Yes please. *(Jeremy pours two tumblers of whisky.)*

JEREMY. Water?

GUY. Ice please. *(Jeremy looks at Guy: wrong answer. He puts some ice into Guy's drink.)*

JEREMY. So what's her name?

GUY. Lauren.

JEREMY. *Lauren.* D'you know, I don't know a single person called *Lauren* isn't that remarkable?

GUY. Not really.

JEREMY. Lauren what, Lauren who?

GUY. Lauren Small.

JEREMY. Small. Is she?

GUY. Not where it matters.

JEREMY. Where's she from?

GUY. Hastings.

JEREMY. Charming. And the parents?

GUY. They have a chain of shops.

JEREMY. Selling what?

GUY. Magazines, newspapers.

JEREMY. A newsagent?

GUY. Chain of them. Several.

JEREMY. Cigarettes and chocolate. Well, people always popping out for a pint of milk. Or *scratch cards*.

GUY. Language.

JEREMY. Where'd she go to school?

GUY. In Hastings.

JEREMY. Day school?

GUY. Comprehensive.

JEREMY. Clever girl, getting to Oxford.

GUY. First in the family.

JEREMY. Goes like the clappers as well, I expect. *(Guy sips his drink.)* In case it helps, Guy, I'm liable to be called back to the Lords any moment, so if you've something to ask, I'd spit it out.

GUY. Right, no, of course. You're very busy. OK, right. It's the — It's the Riot Club. We're back in business. This term.

JEREMY. Yes, I thought it might be that.

GUY. You knew, did you?

JEREMY. Yes.

GUY. James had a call from — James Leighton-Masters, the president —

JEREMY. Yes, I know.

GUY. Had a call from another old member —

JEREMY. Michael Bingham, yes I know.

GUY. Said it's been long enough since —

JEREMY. Yes.

GUY. OK, then you know all of it.

JEREMY. No, please — Go on.

GUY. OK, so we're back, we can start having dinners again, Embargo Relaxum.

JEREMY. On the proviso that you keep it out of the *Daily Mail* this time, right?

GUY. Well yeah. Yeah, but that wasn't about a dinner, though, was it, that story, that was just Toby —

JEREMY. You know what I mean.

GUY. I know we've missed two dinners because of him knobbing about. And you don't get very many, do you, one a term? Not many chances to —

JEREMY. To let rip.

GUY. To make your mark. If you want to be the next president.

JEREMY. Oh, Guy —

GUY. Election's after Christmas, so —

JEREMY. Why d'you want the hassle of being president?

GUY. You know, for the old CV.

JEREMY. Current climate, Guy — employers don't like —

GUY. Not my written CV, obviously. I mean the curriculum of my *actual* vitae. The legend of Guy Bellingfield. So I was thinking I could bring something special to the next dinner. Sort of a trailer. As well as, you know, celebrating the. Glorious return. And, I just, I know that back in the day, you were — you know, you were quite a legend in the club.

JEREMY. Right.

GUY. And I'm a bit, um. Stuck for ideas.

JEREMY. I think you're over-thinking it.

GUY. Just want a bit of inspiration.

JEREMY. It's only a club.

GUY. It's the best club.

JEREMY. Silly student japes, all it is. Letting off steam.

GUY. Please, just. Anything. Please.

JEREMY. Alright, well. Why don't you pitch in with club finances? — Chap did that when I was at college, managed the funds judiciously enough to lay down a cellar of really excellent wine for future dinners, that showed a bit of foresight —

GUY. Yeah, I was thinking of something that might have a bit more of an um, immediate impact. Something with a bit of, you know. Woof.

JEREMY. You know the best thing you could do, Guy, for your *CV*, is ensure this dinner passes pretty uneventfully.

GUY. Right.

JEREMY. Yes?

GUY. Yeah, sorry, OK. Uneventful. Lead by example. The Quiet Man.

JEREMY. Exactly.

GUY. Just easy to get carried away when I grew up on all those stories. Listening to you talk about the club, all the amazing — obviously, that was before things were so —

JEREMY. Sadly, yes.

GUY. God, that one about the — was it a chandelier?

JEREMY. I don't —

GUY. Yeah no, you and the guys — massive food fight, something about a chandelier got caught in the crossfire, shattered everywhere —

JEREMY. One chandelier was hardly a rare occurrence in those days.

GUY. No, yeah, not just *one* —

JEREMY. Christ, some dinners there'd be three chandeliers broken before we even sat down —

GUY. Amazing.

JEREMY. We'd be eating in the dark sometimes.

GUY. Legends.

JEREMY. You know one time — this was bloody funny — we stripped a dining room *totally* bare — wallpaper down, floorboards up — Of course we were all, you know —

GUY. Three sheets to the wind.

JEREMY. More than that.

GUY. Four sheets to the wind.

JEREMY. Took all the electrics out, skirting boards, dado rails, put it all in a huge pile in the middle of the floor —

GUY. Sounds amazing.

JEREMY. Work of genius. Should have seen the owner's face when he saw it.

GUY. Did he go ballistic?

JEREMY. Once we'd given him a blank cheque he thought it was bloody funny, actually. Very nice chap, gave us a lift to the station. Not quite sure how we got there but the next morning we woke up in Vienna.

GUY. Vienna?

JEREMY. Passed out face-down in a box of marzipan.

GUY. Wow. Did you always go somewhere?

JEREMY. After dinner, yes. A jaunt.

GUY. That's it — I should totally arrange a trip — 'cause we usually just end up in a club — I mean wow, this could be seriously —

JEREMY. But I thought you weren't going to —

GUY. Val d'Isère, maybe — bit of drunken skiing —

JEREMY. *Uneventful* we said —

GUY. Or maybe just taxis to the airport — just rock up and take a chance on the next flight out. Have Gold Card, Will Travel. How presidential is that? The Riot Club hits Heathrow.

JEREMY. No, Guy, Guy, wait, think —

GUY. What?

JEREMY. Think about the *dinner*. If you're going to do something.

GUY. What?

JEREMY. Surely what — what happens *inside* the room. Much more important than where you go afterwards. If you're set on leading by example. If you want to make your mark as a leader, not just a, you know, *holiday rep*.

GUY. So …

JEREMY. Well, it's the dinner *itself* — you know, give it some grandeur, some *meaning*. The wine, for example — put some real thought into it: the perfect complement to the ten-bird roast, the perfect Sauternes for the pudding, the —

GUY. Complement to the what?

JEREMY. Pudding.

GUY. No, before that, you said —

JEREMY. Ten-bird roast.

GUY. What's a ten-bird roast?

JEREMY. What it says, isn't it, a bird inside a bird inside a bird and so on.

GUY. Ten different birds. Because there's ten of us in the club, see.

JEREMY. Oh now, there, I'd forgotten.

GUY. Like a metaphor, for — What sort of birds is it?

JEREMY. I don't know, quail, duck, partridge, whatever, you don't cook it yourself I don't know exactly what's in it. But bloody special. I mean this is you connecting yourself to hundreds of years of history.

GUY. A sacrament, almost.

JEREMY. Exactly that — a sacrament. Ten of you, bound together —

GUY. Brotherhood again.

JEREMY. Exactly. Bonding over the meat and the fire.

GUY. And you definitely think that'll work —

JEREMY. It's what they had at the first-ever dinner.

GUY. Savage, OK. So maybe James'd let me take charge of the whole menu — say I'm just trying to help him out — get something properly impressive like a ten-bird roast —

JEREMY. Show you're a man of taste and discernment.

GUY. Awesome president material.

JEREMY. There you go. There's your game plan.

GUY. And then we tear the place apart later.

JEREMY. Guy —

GUY. Jokes, Uncle Jezza — I'm joking. *(Jeremy's phone chimes.)*

JEREMY. Oh god, here we go — *(He holds his phone up to show Guy.)* There's an app now, for the Division Bell.
GUY. Nice.
JEREMY. Look, I — I can't stress enough how important it is that you — If you can be an arbiter of sense and decorum at that dinner, you'll make me, and others in more elevated positions, extremely —
GUY. Don't worry. We'll be good boys, we won't disappoint.
JEREMY. You know what I mean. No fucking about, yes? *(Jeremy's phone chimes again.)*
GUY. Thanks, Uncle Jezza. *(Jeremy leaves. Guy leans back in his chair, looks around the room. Guy's phone rings. He picks up.)* Dimitri, you massive gayer! Listen to this: It's going to be fucking savage. *(Blackout.)*

Scene 2

The private dining room at the Bull's Head Inn, set for dinner, but empty at first. Chris and George enter. George looks around, surprised that the room is empty.

CHRIS. You're the first.
GEORGE. Yeah. Savage.
CHRIS. Well you can tell me if everything's OK — anything you think you'll need you can't see here?
GEORGE. Uh. Yeah. I'm not really the — Not really the right chap.
CHRIS. Been to a wedding?
GEORGE. Uh, no, it's uh. Club regimentals. I mean it's —
CHRIS. Thought you'd be in business suits, more of a pinstripe thing.
GEORGE. Sorry?
CHRIS. Young Entrepreneurs.
GEORGE. Oh yes, yeah. Young Entrepreneurs Club.
CHRIS. I thought that'd be, you know. Entrepreneurs *now*.
GEORGE. Yeah, it's uh. It's retro night. Lovely.
CHRIS. Well, take a pew, make yourself at home. *(George looks at a chair, then looks around the room, at a loss.)*
GEORGE. Yeah, bit weird. On my own. Might go and sit out —
CHRIS. Whatever you prefer. *(Chris ushers George out of the door.)*

GEORGE. Have you got a snug? *(The room is left empty. Moments later, the door opens again and Toby comes in, seething and full of nervy energy. Ed follows behind. Toby is carrying a vintage-looking leather box with a handle — looks like a hat box — and an ornamental sabre in a velvet pouch attached to a sash.)*

ED. Mate, I'm sorry, OK.

TOBY. You're not supposed to move your stuff, fuck's sake.

ED. Is this what you were pissed off about in the cab? You could have said —

TOBY. Looked like Soviet Russia. Like a monk who's taken a vow of no fucking possessions.

ED. Just my computer and the stereo.

TOBY. What, nothing else? Little furry friend?

ED. Yeah, OK.

TOBY. Mr Ted, Big Ted, whatever its name is.

ED. It's just that my brother said —

TOBY. He told you to move your stuff out?

ED. No, he just. Mentioned there'd be something and I knew it'd be either a bedroom-trash or a beasting 'cause it always is, so — Pre-emptive strike.

TOBY. Fucking weasel. Supposed to be awesome. Your entry to the club. They knew soon as they walked in and couldn't find Mr Fucking Snuffles.

ED. Kingsley. Kingsley Bear.

TOBY. Walk in and it's "Where's the bear? Hmm, *nowhere*."

ED. I'm sorry, mate.

TOBY. I'm your sponsor. You fuck it up, it reflects back on me.

ED. Yeah, sorry.

TOBY. Stop saying fucking sorry. Just. Try not to make me look like a twat. *(Ed sits down.)* Mate!

ED. What? *(Ed jumps up.)*

TOBY. You don't sit before the president.

ED. Yeah, I know, I just thought. He's not here yet. No one's here.

TOBY. Dinner starts when you walk through that door. Jesus. *(Toby paces, hands in pockets.)* Where the fuck are they?

ED. Long way to come, isn't it, 'cause of the, um — Radius — *(Ed looks at Toby — he doesn't yet seem appeased.)* Toby, I'm sorry about the bear, OK? He's a family heirloom.

TOBY. *"He"?*

ED. Kingsley Bear has been in my family for like, three generations, a hundred years. If anything happens to him — *it* — I mean my grandmother would go ballistic and she's scary —

TOBY. Why d'you bring it to college?

ED. Family tradition.

TOBY. Fuck's sake.

ED. Look, mate, I get it.

TOBY. What?

ED. I know you've got a rep to repair. I know you're worried the guys are still hacked off at you for the *Daily Mail* thing, but we've all done stupid shit, yeah? And I know you didn't want to be my sponsor, but I'm going to be distressingly awesome tonight. Team Tubes.

TOBY. Mate, fuck, look, tonight's a write-off — They're going to tear me a new one, give me a fucking dregsing, and I'm going to put my head down and take it 'cause once they've done that they can't say anything. But I don't need you cocking about in my eyeline, making it worse, OK? I'm on thin ice here.

ED. Toby, I'm your skates.

TOBY. What?

HARRY. *(Off.)* This one through here? No no, I'll be fine, thank you so much.

ED. Skates, like ice skates —

TOBY. Just stay out my way. *(The door opens and Harry comes in backwards, rather overloaded. He's wearing full fencing gear and carries a large kit bag, with a couple of swords sticking out of it, plus a suit carrier.)*

HARRY. Yeah yeah, I can manage I'll just whack it in a corner. Ooh, hello. Private moment?

TOBY. No one's here yet.

ED. Hi Harry. *(Toby goes into the hat box and takes out a white powdered 1760s-style wig, which he puts on his head during the next.)*

HARRY. Cut the air with a knife.

ED. Or a sword.

HARRY. Oh, it does jokes. *(To Toby.)* Well picked.

TOBY. Didn't pick him. *(Harry hands his kit bag to Ed.)*

HARRY. Ed? *(Harry unzips his suit carrier and takes out his tails. Toby puts on the sash and ornamental sword. Harry notices.)* Wig of shame, nice.

TOBY. You've had a match?

HARRY. I had a match — other chap had a pasting.

TOBY. Varsity?

HARRY. Varsity warm-up. They haven't got a chance.

ED. You won then?

HARRY. I always win. Pasted the captain and then got a blowjob off his girlfriend while he was getting looked at by the physio.

ED. Fuck.

HARRY. Tab shoo!

TOBY. Was she fit?

HARRY. She was from Cambridge. Still, blowjob's a blowjob. Right, can you fuck off for a minute while I get changed?

TOBY. In here?

HARRY. Yeah.

TOBY. Why didn't you dress at college?

HARRY. No time — two hours ago I was still in the rotten Fens. Got dropped off by the minibus.

TOBY. Whyn't you change in the loo?

HARRY. I'm not putting my tails on in the loo, fuck's sake. Just go out in the bar a minute.

TOBY. I'm not going out there.

ED. Toby got wolf-whistled on the way in.

HARRY. So the locals think you're hot.

TOBY. Stand around like a twat when we can't even have a drink yet. *(Chris comes in.)*

CHRIS. Everything alright, gents?

HARRY. Excellent, thank you.

CHRIS. Just looking for James Leighton-Masters.

TOBY. He's not here yet.

HARRY. Leighton's not here yet?

CHRIS. Look like a musketeer.

TOBY. Charades later. *(Toby takes off the sash and sword and leans it against the wall.)*

CHRIS. Alright, well — If he comes in could you point him towards me?

TOBY. Absolutely. *(Chris goes to leave.)*

HARRY. Hi — sorry — actually I could do with a bit of a brush-down. Have you got a room?

CHRIS. A room?

HARRY. You do bed and breakfast, right?

CHRIS. "Restaurant with Rooms," yes.

HARRY. Yes, of course — very good. Could I possibly *borrow* a room — just for half an hour? Don't fancy changing in the loo, you know?

CHRIS. Thing is we're full tonight — you know, Saturday — they're all booked.

HARRY. Oh boo — I mean great, obviously. Are they all here?

CHRIS. Pardon?

HARRY. Have they all arrived, are the rooms actually occupied right now?

CHRIS. Not yet, no.

HARRY. Just if I could possibly pop into one for like, half an hour. Less than.

CHRIS. Thing is, the rooms have got to be ready when they come, so —

HARRY. No no, sure sure. I'm talking about paying, by the way. I mean how much does a room go for? Per night.

CHRIS. Eighty-five pounds.

HARRY. Gosh that's reasonable.

ED. So for half an hour that's what, eighty-five divided by twenty-four —

HARRY. Eighty-five, full whack.

CHRIS. For half an hour?

HARRY. You'd be doing me a favour.

CHRIS. Still have to get it cleaned, though. There's no cleaning staff in until tomorrow —

HARRY. I won't make a mess, I promise.

CHRIS. Well, there's a couple not getting here till nine or so —

HARRY. That's marvellous.

CHRIS. Alright then.

HARRY. Nice doing business with you.

CHRIS. You want to go up now?

HARRY. Yeah, I smell of defeat. Not mine — other chap. *(Harry and Chris go to the door, just as Alistair comes in, roaring like a sergeant major.)*

ALISTAIR. Right then, you cock-sucking arsemonkeys, who's going to get on their knees and give me some fucking ... head — *(He simultaneously clocks that the room is half-empty, and that Chris is there. He holds out his hand to Chris, switching instantly into charming.)* Hi. Alistair Ryle.

CHRIS. Hello.

ALISTAIR. How d'you do.

CHRIS. Very well, thank you.

ALISTAIR. Lovely pub. Alright, chaps?

HARRY. Ryle.

ED. Hi Alistair.

ALISTAIR. *(To Chris.)* Sorry about the, uh —

CHRIS. No no, heard it all before. Should hear Chef when he's cut his finger.

HARRY. Chefs.

ALISTAIR. This part of the original, in here?

CHRIS. Part of the original, yes.

ALISTAIR. Very sympathetic. *(Looks at Harry.)* Tab shoo?

HARRY. Tab shoo. Going to get changed.

ALISTAIR. Excellent, you stink. *(To Chris.)* Good to meet you. *(Chris and Harry go out. Alistair comes into the room, looking around. He sees Toby's wig and points at it.)* Ah, the wig of shame. Fuck this is a long way from town.

ED. Banned from anywhere closer, aren't we, the radius …

ALISTAIR. Taxi driver couldn't find it. Should've hired a minibus, all come together.

ED. Yeah, all rock up together like *Reservoir Dogs*.

ALISTAIR. Excited, Grasshopper?

ED. Yeah.

ALISTAIR. You should be. The Riot Club rides again. *(Alistair lights a cigarette.)*

TOBY. Mate I don't know if we can —

ALISTAIR. Private dining room, that's the point, isn't it? Home from home. *(Ed takes out a packet of cigarettes and lights one. Toby opens a window. Voices are heard coming down the corridor.)* Listen.

HUGO. *(Off.)* Just give it one night, OK? Please. *(Hugo comes into the room, followed by Miles.)*

MILES. It's not the — *(Sees the other boys in the room.)* Forget it, doesn't matter.

HUGO. Evening.

TOBY. Oh look, it's the Magdalen Marys.

ED. Hi Hugo. Miles. *(Hugo takes off his gloves.)*

HUGO. Alliteration, Maitland? Last refuge of the scoundrel.

TOBY. Pompous prick.

HUGO. And again? B-minus. Where's James?

ALISTAIR. Gaffer's not here yet.

HUGO. Huh. Unpresidented.

ALISTAIR. So two new boys. How you feeling?

ED. Awesome. Totes excited.

ALISTAIR. *(To Toby.)* He says totes.

TOBY. Don't say totes, fucking parody of yourself.

ALISTAIR. How'd you like your room makeover, Miles?

HUGO. Al, I wouldn't —

MILES. Well, it was *thorough*.

ED. It was amazing, fucking savage —

TOBY. Mate — doghouse, yeah?

HUGO. Doghouse is already occupied, Toby.

TOBY. Only till the dregsing, mate.

ALISTAIR. Sorry, Milo?

MILES. Didn't quite get the tails-hung-up thing, the symbolism.

ED. What thing?

MILES. Where they hang your tails up on a hanger in the middle of the room. So when you walk in for a second it looks like someone hanged themself.

ED. No way.

ALISTAIR. Just a calling card.

ED. Didn't do that in mine.

TOBY. You haven't got a central light fitting.

ALISTAIR. Why'd you get such a tiny room, anyway? Thought you'd get the set your brother had with the windows onto the quad.

HUGO. "The Montgomery Suite."

ALISTAIR. Awesome quad parties.

ED. Ground floor, mate. Access requirements.

HUGO. Ah. The Monty Suite's been given to a disabled.

ALISTAIR. Jesus fuck.

ED. Well I wish you'd left me a calling card.

MILES. *I* wish they hadn't jizzed all over my fucking stuff. *(The others turn to Miles.)*

HUGO. Milo —

ALISTAIR. Mate?

MILES. Nothing.

ALISTAIR. Is there a problem?

MILES. Well yeah, I —

HUGO. It's fine, he's just —

MILES. I didn't expect someone's semen all over my books.

ED. Mate, it's part of the room trash — that's what happens.

MILES. It's actually really difficult to get off. Paper's porous.

ALISTAIR. Didn't Hugo tell you? This is a club for getting fucked and fucking stuff up, mate.

HUGO. It's a bit more than that, I think you'll —

ED. Don't they trash rooms at Harrow?

MILES. More of a sports club thing.

ALISTAIR. No wait, don't tell me — your mates were all in bands …

MILES. Yeah.

ALISTAIR. … and when you got to Oxford there was this one night in Freshers Week where you were sat in the college bar looking around at all your new friends who grew up in — help me, Tubes —

TOBY. Stockport.

ALISTAIR. Who grew up in Stockport or wherever, when this chap comes and sits next to you —

TOBY. In a smoking jacket …

HUGO. Guys, don't —

ALISTAIR. In a smoking jacket and he says something in Latin — which somehow cuts right to the heart of you …

TOBY. 'Cause he seems to understand exactly — *exactly* — how you're feeling.

ALISTAIR. And then he tells you the story of Lord Riot the famous Libertine. And he feeds you a drink of his favourite vintage Port — private supply — and he tells you he's in Lord Riot's club and you should come along.

TOBY. It's very exclusive. Top secret.

ALISTAIR. *Assentio mentium*: the meeting of minds.

TOBY. And you're exactly the right sort of chap.

ALISTAIR. Hugo Fraser-Tyrwhitt: Operation Pretty Boy.

HUGO. One word for you, Toby: *YouTube*.

ED. Two words. No, sorry —

TOBY. Oh my god, that one last year.

ALISTAIR. Gay Harry Potter?

TOBY. Couldn't afford his tails in the end so Hugo had to drop him.

HUGO. That's not what happened at —

ALISTAIR. Gay Harry Potter.

MILES. I'm not gay, by the way.

ED. It's OK to be gay.

MILES. I know, but I'm not, so — I think there's something fairly gay about wanking in someone's bedroom. I'd also quite like to know whose jizz it is.

ALISTAIR. Hugo?

HUGO. Well, it's. It's one for all and all for one.

MILES. Meaning what?

HUGO. Everyone takes part in the trashing, so in a way it's everyone's jizz.

MILES. You *all* wanked on my books? *(Harry comes in, looking immaculate in his tails.)*

ALISTAIR. Next year *you* get to do it to someone else.

MILES. I don't want to.

HARRY. What are we talking about?

TOBY. You do what the president tells you to do.

HUGO. You don't *have* to.

TOBY. He's supposed to lead by example.

MILES. So James jizzed on my books?

HARRY. Oh no, that was me. Always happy to whack one out for the good of the club. *(Alistair starts to pace the room, looking in the drawers of the sideboard.)*

TOBY. How was the room?

HARRY. Three star.

ED. D'you mess it up?

HARRY. Did a big dump in the loo, got my money's worth. Release the otters!

MILES. Nice.

TOBY. Come on Leighton, let's do this.

HUGO. Has he texted anyone? *(They all whip out their phones and check.)*

TOBY. Nope.

HUGO. No.

HARRY. *(Reading a text.)* Excellent.

TOBY. Mate?

HARRY. No, something else, sorry. Al, did Leighton text you? *(Harry looks at Alistair, sees he's reading from a burgundy leather-look binder that he found in one of the drawers.)* Ooh, what you got?

ALISTAIR. "Your Private Dining Experience at the Bull's Head Inn, Kidsbury."

HARRY. Gosh, are we having an experience?

ALISTAIR. "Guests are invited to choose from three elegant three-course menus."

HARRY. *(Charges towards Alistair.)* Let's have a look. *(Alistair holds the folder away so that Harry can't see it.)*

ALISTAIR. So the game is — Which One Did Leighton Pick?

HUGO. What do we call it, "Meal of Fortune"?

MILES. "Meal or No Meal."

HUGO. Excellent.

ALISTAIR. Here, you be trolley dolly. *(Holds the folder towards Miles.)*

ED. I'll do it.

HUGO. Go on, Miles. *(Miles comes forward and takes the folder from Alistair.)*

ALISTAIR. Good man.

MILES. Um, OK, Menu A:

ALISTAIR. Just a bit of fun till the boss-man gets here.

MILES. Pâté Maison with Melba toast, followed by breast of chicken wrapped in bacon with dauphinoise potatoes and a tarragon jus, then seasonal berry pavlova.

HARRY. It's the '80s retro menu!

ALISTAIR. We are *not* having chicken.

HARRY. What's Menu B? *(Guy comes in, singing LMFAO: "Party Rock Anthem.")*

GUY. Party Rock is in the house tonight / Everybody just have a good time / And we gone make you lose your mind —

TOBY. Bellingfield!

HARRY. Bell-end!

GUY. We just wanna see ya SHAKE THAT — *(Guy does a robotic dance, beeping the tune, but gets distracted after a few moves.)* Where the fuck is Leighton?

ED. Not here yet.

GUY. Sorry I'm late, chaps. Stuff to do.

HARRY. Didn't miss you.

GUY. Harsh. What we doing?

HUGO. Which menu did Leighton pick.

ALISTAIR. Lovely assistant Milo — Menu B?

MILES. Um, tomato gazpacho —

ED. Cold soup. So wrong.

HARRY. Wait wait — Al, isn't gazpacho that red stuff you dip nachos in?

ALISTAIR. No, mate, you're thinking of salsa.

HARRY. Salsa? Why, isn't that a sort of dance?

ALISTAIR. I don't know, you'll have to ask Bellingfield.

GUY. Fuck right off.

TOBY. What's this?

HARRY. Lauren's got Guy going to salsa class.

TOBY. Awesome.

HUGO. Very sensual.

GUY. All in the hips, mate, all about the hips. Anyway, you don't need to —

TOBY. Menu B! Come on!

MILES. Yeah, so gazpacho, then assiette of Denby Farm pork. Three ways.

HARRY. "Three way pork"? That is *filthy*.

ALISTAIR. What's pudding? *(He picks up Harry's fencing foil and starts to mime fighting with it.)*

MILES. Chocolate fondant.

ALISTAIR. Risky. Like it.

HUGO. Menu C?

MILES. Um, carpaccio of beef with parmesan shavings and a rocket salad.

TOBY. What's carpaccio mean?

HUGO. Raw beef, very thinly sliced.

HARRY. That's so gay.

MILES. Then main course is pan-fried sea bream with fennel salad and new potatoes.

HARRY. Gay!

ALISTAIR. Pudding?

MILES. Mango crème brûlée.

HUGO. Burnt cream.

HARRY. So gay. Menu C is the gay menu.

ALISTAIR. So, fingers on buzzers, which one do we think Leighton picked?

MILES. Could have done a mash-up.

GUY. Leighton hasn't picked, though, so the game doesn't really —

ALISTAIR. What? *(Guy comes to Miles and takes the menu out of his hands.)*

GUY. Well, um — fact is, Leighton's delegated the menu this time.

HUGO. Delegated?

GUY. You know, he's got a lot on. OUCA, rowing practice, applying for int —

ALISTAIR and HARRY. Internships.

HARRY. He's the Interninator.

GUY. Chap needed a hand so he uh, he asked me to take care of it.

ALISTAIR. You?

GUY. Yeah.

HUGO. So which one did you pick?

GUY. I didn't —

HARRY. You didn't pick and Leighton didn't pick — what?

GUY. No, it's. Special night, isn't it? Calls for a bespoke approach.

HUGO. It's not one of these menus?

GUY. It's *based* on one of those menus.

HARRY. Which one?

GUY. Well it doesn't matter, 'cause it —

ALISTAIR. Does matter — which one?

GUY. OK, Menu A. *(The others groan.)* Chaps chaps chaps I've *customised* it, so —

HUGO. How?

GUY. Everything's gone a bit more Riot Club.

HUGO. How d'you make chicken a bit more Riot Club?

GUY. Well I don't want to tell you because — just trust me, it's going to be awesome.

HUGO. How d'you *customise* a pavlova?

MILES. Sparklers?

GUY. OK, look, if I tell you about pudding can we put the menus away?

ALISTAIR. Course, yeah.

GUY. So, OK, so it says seasonal berry pavlova on the menu — but we're not from the '80s, yeah, we're from the *now*, so — so I look at that and think OK, work with it, make it celebrate our awesomeness, our back-in-business-ness — ness.

TOBY. So?

GUY. So how d'you make an Eton mess?

HARRY. Tell him he only got into Bristol?

GUY. OK, Eton mess is basically you get a pavlova and then you smash it up with a hammer, right? Far as I'm concerned that's the Riot Club in a pudding. *(The boys think.)* Just wait till you see the main course. *(Chris opens the door to usher someone in.)*

CHRIS. Just through here. *(Dimitri strides into the room, wearing Riot Club tails, plus a scarf and a vintage-style leather helmet and goggles. It's not immediately obvious to the others who he is. He looks like a cross between Mr Toad and Biggles.)*

TOBY. What the f — *(Dimitri puts his goggles on top of his head with a flourish, then stands with his hands on his hips.)*

DIMITRI. Evening chaps. *(The boys laugh, recognising him. Guy goes over to shake his hand/man-hug him.)*

GUY. Dims, mate.

HUGO. Dimitri, you absolute —

DIMITRI. Good to be back, boys. Good to be back. *(Guy puts the menu folder back in a drawer.)*

CHRIS. Um lads, is that smoke I can smell?

ALISTAIR. Smoke? I don't think so. Can anybody smell smoke?

HARRY. Maybe someone outside, I don't know.

CHRIS. If you want to smoke there's a patio at the back.

TOBY. Can't we just blow it out the window?

HARRY. Tubes.

CHRIS. No sign of Mr Leighton yet?

DIMITRI. James isn't here?

HARRY. He hasn't called you?

CHRIS. Nope, nothing. Hoping we'd get started on time, I've got another big party in the restaurant, Ruby Wedding.

GUY. Can I have a word, actually?

CHRIS. Um, yes.

GUY. Guy Bellingfield — we spoke on the phone about the food.

CHRIS. Yes, of course.

GUY. Just wanted a quick word about how you're going to serve it.

CHRIS. Yes, I thought we'd bring it in on a —

GUY. Out of earshot? — So sorry, don't want to spoil the surprise.

CHRIS. Right, course. *(Chris and Guy leave the room.)*

ALISTAIR. Seriously, why would James delegate the food to Bell-end? All he ate at school was potatoes. *(Harry's phone rings.)*

DIMITRI. With ketchup. *(Harry answers the phone.)*

HARRY. Hello? Hi, yeah.

ALISTAIR. The man has no palate.

HARRY. No, we're here. No, not the Bull. The Bull's Head. Kidsbury, yeah. *(Harry leaves the room, putting a cigarette in his mouth as he goes.)*

ED. Thought we weren't supposed to take phone calls.

TOBY. More importantly — Dimitri?

DIMITRI. Yeah?

TOBY. The fuck have you got on your head?

DIMITRI. Just came here on the bike.

ALISTAIR. What bike?

DIMITRI. 1962 Triumph Thunderbird.

MILES. You've got a Thunderbird?

DIMITRI. Bought it yesterday.

ED. Is it like in *The Great Escape*? *(Dimitri takes off his goggles and helmet and puts them on the table.)*

DIMITRI. No, because that's American. This is a classic British bike. 650 cc.

HUGO. How long till you drive it into a pond?

DIMITRI. I'm a good driver.

HUGO. Not going to be a good driver by the end of dinner — how you going to ride it home?

DIMITRI. Whack it in the back of the minibus. *(Guy comes back into the room, tuning back into the conversation.)*

TOBY. Yeah, but sometimes they send a people carrier, Space Cruiser thing — can't fit a motorbike —

DIMITRI. They're not going to send a Space Cruiser.

TOBY. How d'you know?

DIMITRI. 'Cause I booked it myself. It's definitely a minibus.

GUY. You booked it?

DIMITRI. Nothing but the best for my boys.

GUY. How come you booked it?

DIMITRI. You're looking at tonight's official Post-Party Party Starter. Seeing as how we're back with a capital *boom*, James has put me in charge of organising something suitably awesome. Hope you've got your shades, chaps, you're gonna be up till dawn.

HUGO. What, tequila shots on Port Meadow?

DIMITRI. Now did I say we were staying in Oxford?

GUY. Oh my god.

DIMITRI. Got to keep Tubes out of town, haven't we? Away from girls with camera phones.

TOBY. Yeah yeah.

ALISTAIR. So where we going?

DIMITRI. Surprise! Now, who wants a sit on the motorbike?

ED. Me! Me!

HUGO. I'll give it a miss, if you don't mind.

DIMITRI. *(Holds up his keys.)* Your loss. Anyone got a licence?

MILES. Yeah, I have.

HUGO. Have you?

MILES. Yeah.

DIMITRI. Go for your life. *(Hands the keys to Miles. Miles heads out of the door, followed by Toby, Ed, Alistair ... and Hugo.)*

TOBY. Thought you were sitting out.

HUGO. Have a smoke while I'm out there, can't I?

GUY. James gave you the job?

DIMITRI. Well, you know. Volunteered.

GUY. After I told you I was going to talk to him?

DIMITRI. Like you said, elections next term, no harm in helping out a bit, upping one's profile …

GUY. I said that about me, I didn't think you'd be —

DIMITRI. All those ideas you got from your uncle.

GUY. Yeah, ideas *I* got. *(Dimitri shrugs.)* So what, you're getting us all on a flight to Vienna?

DIMITRI. Wait and see.

GUY. Fuck I wish I hadn't told you.

DIMITRI. Why did you? If you didn't want me to have a go as well?

GUY. Because you're my friend.

DIMITRI. Tactical error, mate.

GUY. Yeah, but I didn't think you'd —

DIMITRI. What?

GUY. I didn't think you'd be going for president.

DIMITRI. You think I wouldn't be a good president?

GUY. No, I just —

DIMITRI. Is it 'cause I is Greek?

GUY. No, god. No.

DIMITRI. Jesus, Bellingfield. It's because I'm Greek?

GUY. No, I mean — No, in a lot of ways you're more English than any of us —

DIMITRI. What, it's in the statutes I have to produce four British grandparents, or —

GUY. No.

DIMITRI. You think I can't be president because I'm Greek!

GUY. Mate, mate, really I — I'm not being —

DIMITRI. Game on, mate. Game on. *(Dimitri takes a stack of bank notes out of his pocket and during the following places one bank note under each of the placemats on the table.)*

GUY. What — what you doing?

DIMITRI. All part of the surprise.

GUY. Fuck's sake — *(Alistair and Harry come back in, in high spirits.)*

ALISTAIR. Mate, that is fucking *magnificent*.

HARRY. Those guys knew how to live, you know? Want it, woof it. *(Harry clocks the atmosphere in the room.)* Fuck, it's every time I walk in.

ALISTAIR. *(To Harry.)* Mate, tell the guys what you just told me.

DIMITRI. Bell-end wants to be president.

ALISTAIR. What?

HARRY. We've got a president.

DIMITRI. Bell-end's *campaigning* for next time.

GUY. So are you!

ALISTAIR. Can you stop hacking for two seconds? Villiers.

HARRY. So yeah, I'm talking to this chap I met at Cowes, turns out he's a Riot Club member from back in the roaring '80s. And apparently — at one of the most legendary dinners ever — apparently they hired a girl.

GUY. A girl?

HARRY. Prozzer. Kept her under the table — sucked cocks all night.

ALISTAIR. Fucking hell.

HARRY. Went round under the table, one at a time. Possibly more than one at a time, I mean she's got two hands — you know …

GUY. Oh my god.

DIMITRI. Chlamydia anyone?

HARRY. It's fine, mate, I've booked a clean one, she'll bring paperwork. It's a reputable agency.

GUY. Wait — what — hang on —

DIMITRI. You've *actually* booked one?

HARRY. She'll be here before pudding. *(Alistair, Guy, and Dimitri crease up laughing.)*

ALISTAIR. Isn't that fucking awesome?

DIMITRI. Wait, is this you bidding for president?

HARRY. President? Fuck no. I'm just bringing sexy back. *(Guy and Dimitri glare at each other.)*

ALISTAIR. Does James know?

HARRY. Not the specifics. *(Toby and Ed barrel back into the room, followed by Hugo and Miles — they're all on a motorbike-induced high.)*

TOBY. That is a savage bike, mate.

ED. Savage.

DIMITRI. What d'you think, Huge?

HUGO. Quite stylish, isn't it, as big lumps of metal go.

MILES. So Ed's got an idea where we might be going in the minibus.

ED. Are we going to London? Rock up at Mahiki or —

DIMITRI. No, we're not going to London.

ED. Edinburgh?

DIMITRI. You've all got your passports back at college, yeah?

MILES. God, are we really going somewhere?

TOBY. We're going *abroad*?

DIMITRI. Club tradition, apparently. The after-dinner *jaunt*. Don't know why we got out of the habit.

ALISTAIR. So where we going?

GUY. Vienna.

DIMITRI. We can do better than Vienna.

GUY. Marrakech.

DIMITRI. Nice idea — next time.

GUY. Burma, Cambodia, the Lebanon.

TOBY. Fuck yeah, let's go to the Lebanon!

HARRY. And the mission is to boff someone in a burqa.

HUGO. That's going to take a while, isn't it — get there, presumably buy a ticket —

DIMITRI. We're not going to an airport.

HARRY. Oh mate. Mummy's little runaround?

DIMITRI. Yup.

MILES. What?

HARRY. The Mitropoulos family jet.

ED. A private jet to the Lebanon!

MILES. Fuck.

DIMITRI. We're not going to the Lebanon, OK? We're going somewhere else. *(James hurries in, carrying a rucksack. His shirt is untucked at the front and his bow tie is crooked.)*

JAMES. Sorry, evening chaps, so sorry.

DIMITRI. James, where've you —

ED. Hi James.

JAMES. Numerical reasoning test.

ALISTAIR. On a Saturday?

JAMES. Had to wait for all the others to finish counting on their fingers.

ALISTAIR. Standard.

JAMES. Landlord was being a bit funny — no one's told him we're the Riot Club, have they?

HUGO. He was being funny 'cause you look like you just crawled out of an Oxfam clothes bin. *(Hugo comes over to James and straightens his bow tie for him, while James tucks in his shirt.)*

JAMES. Had to change in the taxi, couldn't do the test in my tails, could I? "Sorry, got to leave early, going to a Riot Cl … *(Sees Chris come in over Hugo's shoulder.)* Young Entrepreneurs dinner." Hi there.

CHRIS. Hi — d'you mind if we get started pretty quick —

JAMES. Not at all. So sorry —

CHRIS. Don't want the timing to be off for your main course.

JAMES. No, absolutely.

CHRIS. Just redoing the toast for your starters. You're all here now, yes?

JAMES. Yes, aren't we? *(Does a quick head count.)* Eight.

DIMITRI. And you.

JAMES. Nine. Who's missing?

GUY. Balf's still in the bar — I'll get him. *(Guy goes out to the bar. The boys start to arrange themselves around the table.)*

CHRIS. And could I possibly take a card to swipe through the machine?

JAMES. Yeah, absolutely. *(Pulls a card out of out his wallet.)*

HUGO. James — which end?

JAMES. *(Points to the end of the table he intends to sit at, then hands a card to Chris.)* Here you go, put it on that one. Social fund.

HUGO. *(Pointing to the seat next to him.)* Milo — you're here.

CHRIS. *(Inserts James' card into a hand-held payment machine and stands near the door, waiting for it to work.)* Future captains of industry, then, are you?

JAMES. Some of us, yeah.

CHRIS. Alan Sugars of tomorrow. *(George and Guy come back in.)*

GEORGE. Here I am chaps, never fear! *(To James.)* Where d'you want me?

JAMES. Up here.

CHRIS. *(To James.)* Just need your PIN number … *(Chris hands the machine to James, who types in his PIN.)*

GEORGE. Um, it's actually just "PIN."

CHRIS. Sorry?

GEORGE. The N stands for "number," it's "Personal Identification Number," so if you say "PIN number," you're actually saying "number" twice.

JAMES. George —

GEORGE. You're saying "Personal Identification Number Number."

DIMITRI. Mate, come on.

JAMES. Have you had a drink?

CHRIS. I'm sorry, I didn't —

GEORGE. *(To James.)* Couple of pints, yeah, but I wasn't in the room yet. *(To Chris.)* Sorry, totally didn't mean that in a rude way, just my father always says it to me, so —

JAMES. *(Hands the machine back to Chris.)* I do apologise.

TOBY. *(To George.)* You're going to be wasted.

GEORGE. Chaps like that offer you a drink, you don't say no thanks.

ED. You could say P.I. Number.

HARRY. Move on, mate.

TOBY. Dims, can Ed sit with you? Please?

ALISTAIR. Get on well with the Wurzels, did you?

GEORGE. Turns out one of them used to work for my father, then he got his own farm, free-range piggies, did terribly well till the economy went, well, tits. Bloody nice chap, too. Shame. *(George finds his place among the boys — they're all standing around the table now, with one space free at the head of the table for James. A slight hush descends. Chris tears off James' receipt and hands his card back to him.)*

CHRIS. There you go, all done.

JAMES. Thanks very much. OK. *(James comes to the table. Chris sees the boys' silence and interprets it as his cue.)*

CHRIS. Right then. Well, evening gentlemen — welcome to the Bull's Head, very glad to have you here this evening, hope you'll have a great night. Please sit down — make yourselves at home … *(The boys all look at James — they can't sit before the president. He considers for a moment, but it's too complicated to explain the protocol to Chris, so he sits. The others are hesitant, looking at James.)*

JAMES. *(Almost under his breath.)* Sit down, guys. *(The others sit.)*

CHRIS. Great. So just a bit of housekeeping before we start serving your dinner. Firstly, this might be a private dining room, but I'm afraid you can't smoke in here. If you do want to pop out there's a patio out the back — you just go out of here, down the corridor to the left and through the fire door. Which is also your fire exit. And there's a lavatory just adjacent, for your private use so you don't have to go through the main bar to access the facilities. Now, hope you're all hungry, no vegetarians around the table, I trust.

TOBY. Villiers only eats pussy.

JAMES. No, there's no vegetarians.

CHRIS. And you want to go straight onto the wine, and leave the champagne until later, yes?

HUGO. We've got plans for the champagne.

CHRIS. Let's get some wine going, then — *(He goes to the sideboard and picks up a bottle of wine already open there.)*

HUGO. *(To Guy.)* Wait, you've chosen the wine already?

CHRIS. *(To Guy.)* Would you care to taste it?

HUGO. Who made you Bottlemeister?

GUY. Goes with the job of the food. Problem?

HUGO. Like asking a builder to do a Fabergé egg.

GUY. D'you want to try it? *(A murmur of anticipation goes around the table.)*

GEORGE. Careful, Huge. *(Hugo looks at the others, narrowing his eyes. They look back challengingly.)*

HUGO. I'll happily. Test it. *(The boys silently watch as Chris goes to Hugo and pours a little wine into his glass.)*

CHRIS. Bought this in specially, we don't normally have it.

GUY. Bespoke service. *(There is almost an intake of breath as Hugo slowly lifts the glass to his mouth. But instead of drinking it, he breathes deeply, inhaling the smell. The boys breathe out, suppressing giggles. Hugo looks at the label on the bottle in Chris' hand.)*

HUGO. Bordeaux? Odd choice.

GUY. Bourgogne. Burgundy.

HUGO. It isn't. *(Chris looks at the label on the wine.)*

CHRIS. Oh heck, sorry, bottles must have got mixed up.

JAMES. What's the problem?

GUY. No no, don't worry — can we just pour the right one instead?

TOBY. What's wrong with that wine?

CHRIS. Yeah, it's still in the cellar, though.

DIMITRI. It's the wrong one.

TOBY. It's wine, isn't it?

DIMITRI. There's a different wine for each course, yeah?

GUY. D'you think we could fetch it, the right one?

DIMITRI. So what's happened is Bellingfield's gone the extra mile and got a pre-dinner wine as well. Because he's *awesome*.

JAMES. What's wrong with the wine, Huge?

HUGO. Just a bit Christmassy for this stage of the meal.

GUY. It's not *for* this stage of the meal, it's for the main course, it'll go perfectly — *(The boys look to James, in need of a decision.)*

HUGO. We should be drinking the right one, shouldn't we, Leighton?

CHRIS. How about I just swap them — serve this now and the other one later?

GEORGE. They're both made out of grapes, right?

GUY. No, but Leighton —

JAMES. Pour it, thank you.

CHRIS. Righto. Sorry about that. *(Chris starts to go around the table, pouring the wine.)*

JAMES. Don't worry, happens to the best of us.

DIMITRI. Oh dear, Bellingfield. Awkward. *(Chris is close to Alistair and jostles his elbow slightly as he leans in to pour his wine.)*

CHRIS. Oh, sorry. *(Alistair takes the bottle from Chris.)*

ALISTAIR. Please — may I?

CHRIS. Want to be a waitress, do you?

ALISTAIR. Sommelier.

CHRIS. OK, well. *(James stands up, ushers Chris towards the door.)*

JAMES. Thanks Chris, that's great.

CHRIS. Your starters'll be along in a minute. Just ask if there's anything else you need.

JAMES. Thank you. Thanks everso much. *(Chris leaves. James shuts the door behind him, then turns around to the others.)* Gentlemen — let's do this.

GEORGE. Hurrah!

TOBY. Fuck yeah! *(They all jump up and stand behind their chairs again. James walks back to the head of the table. The bottle of wine is passed around and empty glasses filled.)*

GUY. Can I just say that was his fuckup about the wine, not mine?

DIMITRI. Mate, it just got a bit complicated.

HUGO. Smells like good wine, it'll be great with the chicken Kiev —

GUY. It's not —

HUGO. Or whatever the big surprise is.

JAMES. OK, starting blocks, chaps, know you're all raring to go. Nice work, Hugo, dodging a scrunch for drinking before the president.

HUGO. I thank you.

TOBY. Come on, let's go!

JAMES. Let's have a bit of order, yeah? Remember this isn't a democracy. *(The boys laugh and quieten down.)* So. Good evening gentlemen, welcome to the Bull's Head. My name's James Leighton-Masters and I'll be your president for this evening. Now, just a bit of housekeeping to go through with you ... *(Various shouts of "Boo!" James pulls out a roll of black bin liners and holds it up.)* before we start on the proper business of the evening: getting chateaued beyond belief. *(The others applaud and whoop, banging the table in delight. James tears one bag off the roll and hands it round the table — they each take a bag and pass it on to the next boy.)* Now, don't forget there's no leaving the room till after dinner — if you do need a piss at any point, you'll notice there's plenty of pot plants. Or you can do it out the window if it's more than a quick wazz. We've been a while in the wilderness, gentlemen, thanks to our bewigged friend over here — who we'll be dealing with later —

HUGO. Not having a dregsing, are we?

33

TOBY. Bring it on. Two pints of milk.

GEORGE. God I've missed this.

JAMES. Two terms without a dinner, boys, two whole terms out in the cold. Let's just say it hasn't been easy. But we've weathered the storm, kept our heads down, our beaks clean, and our faces out of the papers, and we have been handsomely rewarded. Summoned back to the table, to do what we do best.

ED. Yay!

JAMES. Oh, on the proviso that we keep it quiet this time.

ALISTAIR. Boo!

JAMES. "Keep it contained" — I was told — "I'll do what I can," I said, "but hey, all the boys want is to have the evening they *deserve* — and if they want to raise the roof, how could I possibly stop them?" *(The others laugh.)* "How can one man stand against the might of the fucking Riot Club?" *(The others bang the table in agreement.)* There's a new wind blowing, gentlemen. The time for mourning is past, no more beating our breasts and howling at the moon. Now is the time to throw off our chains, to dance footloose upon the earth, to carpe some fucking diem. We've earned tonight, gentlemen. We've earned it. So, in the name of all that is riotous, let us eat till we explode —

GEORGE. Huzzah!

JAMES. Drink till our eyes fall out —

TOBY. Hear hear!

HARRY. Yes!

JAMES. And leave a trail of glorious destruction in our wake. *(The boys clap and cheer.)* Hugo, will you kindly lead the President's Toast? *(Hugo stands up and raises his glass to James.)*

HUGO. We who are about to dine, salute you.

ALL. *Cenaturi Te Salutant.*

JAMES. Gentlemen — imbibe. *(The boys all drink to James, draining their glasses then slamming them down. There's a moment while they take a breath — some of them reel from the alcohol, some reach for the bottles and fill the glasses up again. The party has started.)*

DIMITRI. *(To James.)* Mate, are we singing?

JAMES. Yeah yeah, we're doing it now.

GUY. So patriotic, it's sweet.

JAMES. Hugo? *(The boys prepare to sing. Hugo gives the first note.)*

HUGO. Maaaaaaaah. *(The boys pick up the note and sing the national anthem. Chris opens the door to bring in the starters, but hesitates because of the singing. He nods in approval, then joins in. The boys turn to look, and with the shock their singing peters out. Chris is left singing "God Save the Queen" on his own, with a plate of pâté de foie gras in each hand. Blackout.)*

Scene 3

Later. The boys are finishing their pâté. George is standing up.

DIMITRI. Don't know, just a slightly odd texture.

GUY. If you don't like it, don't eat it.

DIMITRI. Just a bit gritty, that's all.

JAMES. I don't think it's gritty.

GUY. Ironic really. Cousins in Greece eating *actual grit* right now.

ED. Have they run out of houmous?

TOBY. Debt crisis, you wad.

GEORGE. I'll eat it. Woofed mine down already. Yum, Bellingfield. *(Dimitri and George swap plates.)*

DIMITRI. Just had better, that's all.

GUY. What, wrapped in a vine leaf?

HUGO. *(To Guy.)* Will you be enlightening us as to the metaphorical import? Or is it just "the Riot Club in a pâté"?

DIMITRI. What's this?

HUGO. Guy's menu. Everything's got a special symbolic significance.

DIMITRI. Oh, this is classic.

GUY. Foie gras: it's hedonism, isn't it — the ultimate extravagance. That's what we stand for.

DIMITRI. Classic.

ED. I thought that was caviar.

DIMITRI. Don't they force-feed them?

GUY. What?

DIMITRI. The geese, yeah? Force-feed them till they get massively distended livers?

HUGO. Gavage.

DIMITRI. Awesome metaphor, mate.

GEORGE. Uh, chaps, still waiting here.

35

JAMES. Guys, yeah, sorry — everyone finished? Balf's doing the Lady Anne. *(The boys quieten down and listen. Miles goes to stand up, but Hugo stops him.)*

HUGO. We sit for this one.

GEORGE. Gentlemen: *(George raises his glass.)* the Lady Anne.

HUGO. Is that it?

GEORGE. What?

HUGO. You're not going to say anything about her beauty or —

GEORGE. Not so good with the wordy stuff, I —

ED. Who's Lady Anne?

HUGO. Lord Riot's girlfriend, mistress whatever, the one he was in love with.

JAMES. Don't worry about it Balf, it's fine.

HUGO. No, it's — if it weren't for Lady Anne, the club wouldn't exist, would it? *(Dimitri goes to stand up.)*

DIMITRI. I'll do it.

JAMES. Not this one, Dims.

DIMITRI. What, too dusky for you?

MILES. Why can't Dimitri do it?

ALISTAIR. Have to be titled.

GUY. God, protocol, Dims.

ED. I thought *Lord Riot* started the club.

GEORGE. Guys I would dearly love to eat this pâté.

HUGO. Do the toast properly, then. Extemporise.

ED. So the club was started by a *girl*?

HUGO. Riot's *friends* started the club to honour his memory.

JAMES. Sit down, Balf.

HUGO. No. It's supposed to be a moving tribute to her finer qualities, yes?

GEORGE. OK, um. Well. She was very very beautiful and very very nice and I think any of us would have been lucky to have the opportunity to fight a duel for her, um, honour, though I think I probably wouldn't have got a second glance off her, being as I am, a bit of a tool.

HARRY. Oh, mate.

GEORGE. The Lady Anne.

ALL. The Lady Anne. *(They all drink the wine down in one and slam the empty glasses down on the table. They reach for the bottles and fill the glasses up again.)*

ED. So Lord Riot was never *in* the Riot Club?

TOBY. Fuck's sake what's wrong with you —

MILES. When did the smashing start? *(Chris and Rachel come in.)*

CHRIS. We clear these plates out of your way, lads?

JAMES. Absolutely. *(Several of the boys stand up as Rachel comes into the room.)*

CHRIS. This is Rachel — she'll be helping me out serving you this evening.

HARRY. Hello.

JAMES. Hello Rachel.

RACHEL. Please, you don't need to —

ED. Hi Rachel.

GUY. Sorry, Dimitri would like to know if you've got any taramasalata hanging about.

GEORGE. Yeah, chap needs his fish eggs, d'you have any?

JAMES. Guys —

CHRIS. Um, Rachel, have we got any taramasalata?

RACHEL. No Dad.

GEORGE. Or any euros?

ED. Dad! Is he your dad?

CHRIS. Rachel's my daughter, yes.

GUY. We need pitta bread and euros!

RACHEL. It's a joke, Dad — I think he's Greek.

TOBY. Yeah, jokes.

DIMITRI. Sorry, Rachel — trouble with Guy is he's *hilarious.*

JAMES. Did we mention the pâté was excellent?

HUGO. Exemplary!

CHRIS. Thanks very much. Michael will be chuffed. The chef.

HARRY. So, father and daughter team, then?

RACHEL. Yeah, Frank and Nancy Sinatra.

ED. Like Miley Cyrus and. Miley Cyrus's dad.

CHRIS. Just passing through, aren't you love? — She's got a degree.

RACHEL. Oh, everyone's got a degree, Dad —

CHRIS. Job market, you know?

JAMES. Yeah, tough, isn't it?

CHRIS. I mean you'd think she'd just walk into something, with a first.

RACHEL. *(To Toby.)* You finished?

TOBY. *(Blinks, flustered.)* Wuuurm — I mean yeah.

HUGO. A first? Felicitations.

GEORGE. Which college, Rachel?

RACHEL. Newcastle.

GEORGE. Is that near LMH?

HARRY. Mate, some people go to universities that aren't Oxford.

GEORGE. Oh yeah.

HARRY. Sorry, he's had a very sheltered life.

CHRIS. She could have gone to Oxford, didn't want to.

JAMES. Full of idiots like this lot, isn't it?

HARRY. What d'you read?

RACHEL. Modern Languages.

HARRY. You'd need to up there, wouldn't you?

RACHEL. Yeah, French, Spanish, and Geordie.

ED. Geordie Studies!

GUY. *(Crap Geordie accent.)* Weer's me Newky Brown?

MILES. I'm sorry about this.

GEORGE. That was really excellent pâté — I had two, so —

CHRIS. Thank you.

GUY. Rachel, did you drink Newky Brown?

RACHEL. Only for breakfast. *(She leans in to pick up Harry's plate.)*

HARRY. Chanel. Coco Mademoiselle.

RACHEL. Yes. Well done. *(Chris and Rachel are finished collecting the plates.)*

CHRIS. OK, your main course'll be along in a minute.

DIMITRI. What's the main course? *(Chris goes to answer, and Guy has to cut him off.)*

CHRIS. It's a —

GUY. SURPRISE! Still a surprise, remember.

CHRIS. Yes, of course, sorry.

JAMES. Don't mind them — all a bit high-spirited.

ED. Bye Rachel. *(Chris and Rachel leave. Guy gets up to close the door behind them.)*

GUY. Nice try, Dims.

DIMITRI. I'm nearly coming in my pants from the expectation.

JAMES. *(Stands up.)* Right chaps — Banbury Toasts, while we're still upright.

ED. That girl is tasty.

GUY. No chance mate, if Villiers saw her first. *(The others all stand.)*

ED. He's already had a blowjob today.

JAMES. *(Points at Harry, accusingly.)* Yeah, and scrunching Harry Villiers for sharking the waitress. *(The boys jeer. Harry holds up his glass.)*

TOBY. No sharking at the table.

HARRY. The *delectable* waitress! *(The boys laugh and chant "scrunch scrunch scrunch" as Harry drains his glass and then refills it.)*
ED. Legend. *(James raises his glass.)*
JAMES. OK, our next toast — which is to the many, many great men who have sat around this table before us. Gentlemen, raise your glasses to the dead members.
ALL. Dead members. *(They down their drinks, then fill the glasses again.)*
DIMITRI. You've got a dead member, haven't you, Leighton? Or is it just in a coma 'cause you haven't used it in so long?
JAMES. Only 'cause your mum's been out of the country.
GUY. No shortage of penis-action once the prozzer gets here.
GEORGE. Anyone got some WD-40 for Leighton?
JAMES. Once the what gets here?
HARRY. The prozzer.
JAMES. You booked a prozzer?
HARRY. Ho yus.
JAMES. Fucking hell.
HUGO. What's he done?
MILES. I think he's hired a prostitute.
HARRY. Thought we could stick her under the table, go round one at a time.
ALISTAIR. What time's she booked?
HARRY. Half past soon.
ED. That is savage.
HUGO. Oh Villiers, that's so you.
HARRY. She'll be under the table. I asked her to bring a false moustache for when she does you.
JAMES. Mate, are you serious? This is —
TOBY. This is fucking awesome!
GEORGE. Oh my wow.
JAMES. We're supposed to be keeping it —
HARRY. What?
JAMES. Michael Bingham — I promised him we'd, you know, rein it in a bit.
HARRY. There's precedent — acceptable in the '80s.
ED. Who's Michael Bingham?
GUY. Ex-member. Keeps an eye on stuff.
ALISTAIR. God, the fucking alumniati. You've had your moment, guys.
JAMES. Yeah, but —

GUY. Don't be a pussy, Leighton.

HUGO. Sure it's not too late to cancel.

HARRY. Reclaiming our heritage, isn't it?

ALISTAIR. The evening we deserve, you said.

DIMITRI. Yeah, back in business, carpe some fucking diem.

ALISTAIR. Look, Bingham's never going to know, is he?

HARRY. It's a discreet agency, I did check. Who's going to find out? Are we celebrating or are we celebrating?

DIMITRI. *I'm* celebrating.

JAMES. OK, OK. Fuck it, what they don't know won't hurt them. *(There's a general eruption of jollity.)*

HARRY. Excellent.

GEORGE. Huge — Tyrwhitt — Hugo — *(To James.)* Is Hugo doing the Members Ex —

JAMES. Yeah. Guys — guys — listen up — Time for the most important toast of all, the Members Extant. Hugo Fraser-Tyrwhitt.

MILES. We're toasting *ourselves*? *(The others applaud. Hugo bows, enjoying the attention.)*

HUGO. Thank you, thank you. So to put this in context for our newest initiates, back in the very olden days the pause between courses were typically taken up with the recital of poetry, a habit we've rather fallen out of —

ED. Poetry?

HUGO. Wrote it themselves, yes. Imagine a sonnet written by Villiers.

HARRY. "Shall I compare thee to a bummer's arse?"

HUGO. If Villiers had any wit. On this of all nights, I see no reason why we shouldn't take a turn for the *iambic*, since we're dwelling on past as well as future glories. Permit me, then, to summon the spirit of another age, one of wine, women, and *soliloquy*. *(Hugo assumes a dramatic pose and begins to recite his poem.)*

> Once more unto the drink, dear friends, once more,
> And give a roar for all our English drunk.
> In peace there's nothing so becomes a man
> As Milo's sweetness and sobriety;
> But when the call to drink rings in his ears,
> He'll imitate the action of the Tubester;
> Stiffen the member, summon up the sword,
> Disguise understanding with hard-drinking rage;
> Then look like Guy with terrible aspect;
> Burning eyes 'neath the wiggage of the head

Like the George Balfour; let the brow o'erwhelm it
As fearfully as does a Grecian frown
O'erhang and jutty poor Dimitri's face,
Steeped in the wild and wanton ouzo.
Now be like Ryle and stretch the gullet wide,
Be Harry the brave, and hold up every sabre
To its full height. On, on you noblest Riot,
Whose blood is fet from vodka eighty-proof!
Drinkers that, like so many Old Etonians
Have in these parts from morn till even drank,
Then drank some more for love of Leighton.
Dishonour not dead members; now attest
That Knights like our Lord Riot did beget you.
Be envy now to clubs of weaker blood,
And teach them how to drink. The game's afoot!
Pour out the spirits, and with glasses charged
Cry, "God for Harry, Dimitri, and Alistair, James, Toby,
     Edward, Milo, Hugo, Guy, and George!"
(Hugo ends on a roar and the others break into rapturous applause.
Hugo has a big drink, feeling great about himself. He sits down and
the others slap him on the back, joyfully. The door is flung open and
Chris comes in wheeling a trolley, on top of which is a huge roast.)

GUY. Whoa — whoa — Gentlemen, pray silence for the main course.

GEORGE. Oh my Christ. What is that?

ALISTAIR. It's magnificent.

CHRIS. Bit of a monster, isn't it?

JAMES. *What* is it?

GUY. What you're looking at, gentlemen, is a *ten-bird roast.*

CHRIS. Actually, it's a —

GUY. Shake my hand. *(Chris shakes Guy's hand.)* Good man.

CHRIS. Thanks. Thank you.

DIMITRI. It's not grotesque at all.

ED. What's a ten-bird roast?

GUY. Exactly what it says — a bird inside a bird inside a bird inside
a bird. Etc.

HARRY. Roasted.

HUGO. It's what they ate at the first-ever dinner.

GUY. Exactly — heritage.

HUGO. *(To Miles.)* What d'you think?

MILES. Pretty impressive.

GUY. 'Cause there's ten of us, you see. It's one for all — i.e. one bird for each of us — and all for one — i.e. those ten birds bound together in the heat of the fire — the fire being our recent adversity — bound together in the heat of the adversity-fire into one entity. I.e. the club.

DIMITRI. Impeccable logic there. What birds is it?

GUY. Well, chicken for a start —

GEORGE. Must be something tiny in the middle or you've nowhere to go.

ED. Quail maybe?

HARRY. Poussin?

CHRIS. Woodcock, isn't it?

GEORGE. Woodcock are tiny. Bugger to shoot at.

DIMITRI. Seriously, what birds is it?

CHRIS. Biggest turkey we could find, and the others are all inside.

ALISTAIR. So what, you just stuff them inside each other?

DIMITRI. Tell me what the other birds are.

CHRIS. Some of them get deboned.

GEORGE. Yeah, they'd have to be.

DIMITRI. I think we'd all like to know, Guy.

GUY. God, OK, it's um, *(He counts on his fingers.)* poussin —

MILES. No, woodcock.

GUY. Woodcock. Duck, chicken, goose, grouse, quail, partridge, turkey um um. *Pigeon*, pheasant, that's ten.

CHRIS. It's not a grouse, it's a guinea fowl.

GEORGE. Ah, guinea fowl, yes.

CHRIS. Except we didn't —

GEORGE. So they're deboned and then wrapped around each other, are they?

TOBY. Spatchcock!

GEORGE. What, mate?

TOBY. No, just that, really.

ALISTAIR. Bet the Stoics never had a ten-bird roast.

HARRY. It really is incredible. *(To Guy.)* Well done, mate.

CHRIS. Took two of us to get it sewn up and in the oven.

HUGO. Hats off, Guy, that's no chicken Kiev.

CHRIS. *(To Guy.)* Now I know you specified ten birds —

TOBY. When we cut through it, will it be like rings of meat?

GUY. You'll see. What d'you reckon, Balf?

GEORGE. It's amazing. Bellingfield — it's amazing.

GUY. Alright, is it, Leighton?

JAMES. Bravo, mate. Good work. *(Chris looks around at the others.)*
CHRIS. OK, who's going to carve? *(Harry stands up.)*
HARRY. How about I do it … *(He takes the ornamental sabre and draws it with a flourish.)* with this? *(The boys clap, cheer, and bang the table. Blackout.)*

Scene 4

Later. The boys are finishing their main courses, with the remains of the enormous roast on the table in front of them. The atmosphere is considerably more subdued than before. Toby lifts his plate and smashes it down on the edge of the table.

TOBY. *Nine* fucking birds.
GUY. Yeah, OK, but. It's still nine birds.
TOBY. How is a nine-bird roast awesome?
GEORGE. I think it's delicious.
MILES. You're eating giblets.
GEORGE. Best bit. Delicious.
ALISTAIR. Did he tell you it was only nine birds?
GUY. No, he didn't.
ALISTAIR. Then we should complain.
MILES. Are we sure we counted right?
HUGO. Balf knows his game.
GEORGE. Definitely nine birds there.
ED. Unless there was, like, a blue tit smashed up in the stuffing.
ALISTAIR. If he made me eat a blue tit, I'll fucking sue.
JAMES. Come on — it was totally cool.
DIMITRI. Well, ninety per cent cool.
GUY. What do they eat in the Lebanon? Squirrel kebab?
DIMITRI. We're not going to the fucking —
JAMES. What's this?
DIMITRI. Nothing, it's —
JAMES. We're going to the Lebanon?
TOBY. Nine birds!

DIMITRI. I mean, let me get this right, Bell-end — if the birds are *us*, actually we're saying one of us doesn't exist, so who's the invisible guinea fowl, who's that supposed to be?

GUY. OK, so maybe the *metaphor's* gone a bit wobbly, but —

DIMITRI. Mate, without the metaphor, it's just a pile of meat.

JAMES. It's seriously not that big a thing.

DIMITRI. It sort of is, though. Bellingfield planned this extremely carefully — ten birds, one for each of us — What that man's done is pissed all over Bell-end's beautiful plan. He's basically made Guy's best idea *ever* into something pretty disappointing.

GEORGE. Hey, what's pudding going to be?

MILES. A ten-cake cake.

ALISTAIR. It's not just the metaphor, it's the principle. We paid for a ten-bird roast, we didn't get a ten-bird roast.

GEORGE. Yeah, Bellingfield — what's for pudding? Is it a ten-cake cake?

JAMES. It fed all of us.

GUY. No, pudding's just — Just normal.

JAMES. There was fuckloads of meat — I mean look at all the leftovers. They'll be doing game pie for weeks off that.

ALISTAIR. And we're happy with "good enough," are we?

JAMES. That was a fucking decent roast, it was —

GUY. It was a fucking decent roast, thank you.

ALISTAIR. Get the landlord in, get him to explain himself.

GEORGE. Guys, let's not have a fight about —

DIMITRI. I'm happy to speak to the guy if you want me to.

JAMES. If that's what you want to do, fine.

HUGO. No no no no, it should be the president who complains.

DIMITRI. Really, I can do it — Leighton clearly doesn't *care*.

HUGO. Doesn't have the gravitas if it isn't the president.

JAMES. Guys, I *do* care, course I care. It's our night.

ALISTAIR. Well is it or isn't it?

HUGO. If it's our night, we should get our way.

GUY. Oh god it's just a pile of meat.

TOBY. Gauntlet's down, mate.

JAMES. Fine — fine. Picking up the gauntlet. If that's what the evening needs.

DIMITRI. Next time he comes in, yeah?

ED. When they bring in the ten-cake cake. (*James salutes.*)

JAMES. For King and Country.

HUGO. Oh Captain my Captain!

JAMES. *Brigadier*, thank you.

DIMITRI. How about something to help you over the top?

JAMES. What?

DIMITRI. You know, get on the *snow patrol*.

TOBY. Weaponise!

HARRY. Drop the C-bomb.

ED. What are they talking about?

GUY. *Coke*, you douche.

JAMES. Yeah yeah — George?

GEORGE. Right, yeah, um. Yeah, about that —

JAMES. What?

GEORGE. Yeah, um. Bit of a problem with the old, um, procurement actually.

TOBY. Oh *what*?

JAMES. It's your turn, mate —

GEORGE. Yeah, well I tried, OK. Managed to find this chap in the first year, yeah, who knows this chap he gets it off in Blackbird Leys but he said I had to get it myself —

ALISTAIR. But you didn't get it?

GEORGE. Look I had to leave the beagling dinner early, yeah, which *really* isn't the done thing, then I had to wait on this bench for ages and it was bloody cold, all these people staring at me —

DIMITRI. Mate, you didn't go to Blackbird Leys in your plus fours, did you?

HUGO. Foolhardy.

GEORGE. So this quite smelly gentleman comes up and starts chatting to me and I assume it's my chap because he looks like a drug dealer —

DIMITRI. Drug dealers just look normal, mate.

GEORGE. Yes well I know that *now*, so — So I'm really not sure of the protocol but eventually he cuts to the chase at which point I realise he's not the chap I'm supposed to meet, he's actually a sort of, a sort of a —

GUY. Tramp.

GEORGE. You know, a homeless. So we're chatting and he —

DIMITRI. Does this story have an end or just a middle?

GEORGE. I got mugged, OK?

HUGO. Oh mate.

GEORGE. Asks me if I've got any change. And I said. I said "I'm really sorry, I've only got notes."

DIMITRI. "I've only got notes"? What did you expect?

GEORGE. Yes, OK, yes. Anyway, he pulls a knife and demands I give him my — my wallet. Then the actual dealer actually turns up and yes, Dims, he did look perfectly normal, then when I told him I hadn't got the money anymore he looked very cross and did some shouting and then I did some running away.

TOBY. Fuck.

GUY. No sniffy.

HUGO. Chaps, George got mugged.

HARRY. Has anyone got some? Dims?

DIMITRI. Riot Club's my night off from being powder-provider, mate.

TOBY. What do we do, Leighton?

JAMES. OK, guys, we'll just have to, um. Not.

ALISTAIR. Oh this is fucked.

HARRY. Hey, Balf — the farmers in the bar you were talking to?

GEORGE. Yeah?

HARRY. Go and see if they've got any ketamine or something.

GEORGE. What?

HARRY. You know, for horses.

HUGO. Or we could stop behaving like —

HARRY. Seriously Balf — go and get some ket from the farmers.

GEORGE. They're not going to have any on them.

HARRY. They might.

GUY. Go on, Balf.

GEORGE. No they won't because a) why would they bring horse tranquiliser to the pub, and b) even if they did it'd be liquid 'cause you can't get a horse to snort something, and 3) I don't see why we have to take drugs anyway, I don't even like it — coke doesn't even really do anything except make you feel rotten the next day. I think I'd rather have a pint, actually. *(The door opens and Rachel comes in, carrying a tray.)* Seriously.

RACHEL. Just come in to clear. Everything alright for you?

JAMES. Yes. Fine, thank you. *(She puts the tray down and starts to collect the main course plates onto it.)*

DIMITRI. Leighton?

JAMES. Yes, OK. Hi — Sorry, Rachel, isn't it?

RACHEL. Yeah.

JAMES. Is your dad around, Rachel?

RACHEL. He's sorting out the Ruby Wedding. D'you need to speak to him?

JAMES. No no, don't worry — I'll have a chat with him later.

DIMITRI. Talk to Rachel about it.

RACHEL. What?

JAMES. I said I'd talk to Chris, not —

MILES. We can speak to you, since you're here, Rachel.

JAMES. No, mate, I said I'd —

HARRY. Rachel's our mate, you can talk to her.

ALISTAIR. What have you got to say to the lady, *brigadier*?

RACHEL. Sorry, is there a problem?

JAMES. Right, yeah. Yeah, the guys would like to complain about —

DIMITRI. No, you — *you'd* like to complain.

JAMES. OK, yeah. Sorry about this, know this isn't your fault, but we'd like to complain about the fact of the um, the ten-bird roast, because it only had nine birds in it, actually. By our reckoning.

RACHEL. Really? I told him you were all too pissed to notice.

JAMES. Sorry?

RACHEL. He was worried about it earlier, said the butcher let him down, couldn't get hold of any guinea fowl this week but didn't tell him till the last minute. I said I couldn't imagine anyone being bothered to count the rings on it.

JAMES. No, well. I'm surrounded by pedants.

GEORGE. I'm not a peasant!

JAMES. *Pedant*, not peasant.

GEORGE. I've got *patent*.

JAMES. I know, I said *pedant*.

HUGO. Could have got a guinea fowl out of Harry's back garden.

ALISTAIR. His back garden's most of Warwickshire.

HARRY. Honestly — it's not *most of.*

JAMES. It's just that when we arrange something, we kind of expect to get it, you know?

DIMITRI. When we're paying for it.

RACHEL. I'm sure he'll have tried to tell you about it.

JAMES. He actually kind of didn't.

RACHEL. OK, is anyone still hungry? Did anyone not have enough to eat? 'Cause I could make you an omelette?

ALISTAIR. The thing is, Rachel, we're not your normal punters —

JAMES. These chaps have eaten in some of the finest restaurants in the country.

DIMITRI. The world, mate.

RACHEL. *(Laughs.)* So what you doing in Kidsbury, then? Oh yeah.

Young Enterprise. *(Rachel picks up the tray.)* I'll tell Chris what you said. *(She realises she can't get out of the door without putting the tray down again, but James leaps up to open it for her.)*

JAMES. Other than the numbers issue, I mean what there was of it was lovely, so you know —

RACHEL. Yeah. You might want to keep the noise down a bit. *(She goes out. James shuts the door behind her and turns back to look at the table.)*

GEORGE. Boo. *(James sits down.)*

GUY. Well that could have gone better.

JAMES. It's fine, it's fine.

TOBY. Mate, you got rinsed.

JAMES. No I didn't.

GEORGE. Chaps chaps, come on.

TOBY. Leighton got totally fucking rinsed. "Other than the numbers issue it was lovely" — what the fuck?

JAMES. OK, fine. *(Stands up.)* Point of order: anyone fancy a dregsing?

TOBY. What, now?

JAMES. Suddenly in the mood for one.

GUY. Seconded!

HUGO. Do we have to?

HARRY. Thirded!

TOBY. Well fucking come on then, let's get it done. *(Stands up in preparation.)* OK, so once this is over you can't take the piss anymore, yeah? Total fucking moratorium. And no chewing gum, no jizz, Villiers —

JAMES. Just a minute, Tubes. Sit down a sec.

TOBY. What? *(James pulls a piece of paper out of his pocket.)*

JAMES. Something to read out first.

TOBY. What, what is it?

JAMES. Just something to put all this in context, that's all. For the new boys. *(Reads:)* "Dear Mr. Bingham. I am writing to express my great regret for recent events for which — " *(Toby leaps from his chair, trying to grab the piece of paper from James, but George and Dimitri jump up and pull him away.)*

HARRY. Oh mate.

TOBY. That's private, that's a private —

JAMES. Yeah, wasn't going to do it but you've pissed me off, so —

TOBY. Fuck.

JAMES. This is a letter Tubes wrote back in — *(Consults the letter.)* March this year. So shortly after the shitstorm.

ALISTAIR. How'd you get it?

JAMES. Just requested a copy for the archives.

HUGO. Get Tubes to read it.

GUY. Yeah, you read it.

TOBY. Fuck's sake.

ED. Go Tubes!

HARRY. Don't let him grab it.

JAMES. I'll hold it, yeah. You read — from there —

TOBY. "On the night in question, myself and a number of other Riot Club members attended Spires, a nightclub in Oxford."

JAMES. No, next bit, that bit

TOBY. "I took it upon myself to procure some female company for the party, and invited two young ladies to join us in the VIP area. One of whom was Clare Sweet."

HARRY. *Total* bitch.

GUY. What kind of a name is *Clare Sweet*?

TOBY. Bit like *Lauren Small*, isn't it?

HUGO. Read, Tubes.

TOBY. "I spent the next portion of the evening in private conversation with Ms Sweet, during which contravened club secrecy rules."

GEORGE. Boo!

TOBY. "I am also aware by report that I may have said some wrong-headed things which caused the club to seem ridiculous."

HARRY. What, like "I love the sound of breaking glass"?

MILES. Oh my god, did he say that?

DIMITRI. Yeah, then he held his glass out and dropped it on the floor.

MILES. Did it break?

DIMITRI. Nope. Fell on a scarf. *(The boys laugh.)*

TOBY. "I had no idea that Ms Sweet had begun to record our conversation on a mobile phone. Nothing in Ms Sweet's demeanour — "

HARRY. Sorry, Tubes, I think someone's phone's ringing?

GUY. Oh, that's me, sorry, just got a new ringtone … *(Guy takes his phone out of his pocket — The ringtone is a sample of Toby's voice over and over, saying, "I love the sound of breaking glass," and "Total carnage.")*

TOBY. "I tried to take" — Fuck you, Bellingfield — "I tried to take the audio clip off YouTube as soon as" — OK, there's another phone going — *(Harry pulls out his phone, playing a sample of Toby saying, "All the way to Chunderland," over a dance beat. It stops quite suddenly and Harry fiddles with the phone.)*

HARRY. Wait — fuck — call me again, Dims. *(Dimitri does so.*

Harry's phone rings again and the boys dance along to the ringtone for a moment.)

TOBY. OK, whatever. Oxford student, *Daily Mail*, picture of the Prime Minister, you know the rest.

JAMES. Just want the guys to hear the final paragraph.

TOBY. Jesus.

GUY. Take it to the bridge, Tubes.

TOBY. "I know that I made a grave error of judgement and deeply regret that my actions have brought the club into disrepute."

HUGO. Oh god, I can't bear it

TOBY. "My error stemmed mostly from a feeling of pride at being a member of the club, which I struggled not to share. I have taken a long hard look at myself and have — "

GEORGE. Oh no no no —

TOBY. "Have suffered a number of sleepless nights thinking about — "

HUGO. Oh god Leighton make it stop —

JAMES. Move to a dregs?

GUY. Seconded.

HARRY. Thirded.

DIMITRI. Fourthed.

JAMES. Gentlemen, please dregs your glasses. *(The boys grab their half-full wine glasses.)*

GEORGE. God, I love a dregsing.

MILES. What do I do?

ALISTAIR. Put something in your wine — snot, spit, whatever — *(The boys individually adulterate their own glass of wine, variously adding snot, saliva, phlegm, salt and pepper, torn-up bread, earth from a nearby plant pot, ear wax, candle wax, etc. Harry turns away from the table and unzips.)*

TOBY. Guys, clemency, please?

HARRY. Thank fuck — I needed a piss anyway.

HUGO. Oh Villiers, put it away.

TOBY. Mate please don't piss in it —

HARRY. Oops I'm pissing in it.

ED. I've just put a little bit of salt in mine, so —

JAMES. Ready Tubes? One minute on the clock to get round the table. Everyone done?

MILES. Hang on a sec — *(Finishes crumbling a piece of bread into his glass of wine, then looks around for something more.)* Wait a sec — *(He grabs a bowl of potpourri from the sideboard and sprinkles some of it into his glass, then stirs it with a spoon and sits back, satisfied.)* OK.

JAMES. Toby — dregs! *(The boys clap in time and shout "dregs dregs dregs" as Toby moves around the table, drinking down each dregsed glass of wine. After five glasses, Toby clings to the back of the chair, doubled-over, nearly falling.)*

TOBY. Bag — *(The boys hold out a bag for him, which he vomits into. Toby pulls himself up again and continues around the table, drinking another two glasses, after which he falls onto his knees.)*

HARRY. Try and finish it, mate. *(Toby pulls himself up again and drinks one more glass. He falls to his knees again and holds out his hand for the next glass, but Alistair pulls it out of his reach.)*

ALISTAIR. No.

TOBY. I can do it —

ALISTAIR. No, mate —

TOBY. Come on, want to get it done —

ALISTAIR. Just — what are we doing? What are we doing?

DIMITRI. Don't suddenly get all Save The Children, Ryle.

ALISTAIR. I'm not — I'm just — Hasn't he taken enough shit for this?

JAMES. He has to be punished.

ALISTAIR. For what? For being proud of the club? Why shouldn't he —

JAMES. He *talked* about it.

ALISTAIR. Didn't lie, did he? Now fucking look at him —

JAMES. Sorry, what you saying, mate.

ALISTAIR. I'm saying — I don't know — I'm saying — I mean isn't that exactly what they want? People just waiting for us to put a foot wrong so they can take the piss, yeah? I mean doesn't it feel a bit like the world's queuing up to shit on us? You know, the wrong wine, fucking gritty pâté — sorry Bell-end but it was shit —

GUY. It wasn't shit —

ALISTAIR. Leighton late for his own dinner because he's doing a maths test for a fucking *internship*? Jesus, when did that happen? Fucking *begging* for jobs.

JAMES. We're not being shat on, not begging for jobs it's — *(Harry's phone rings. Ten sets of ears prick up.)*

HARRY. Gentlemen — it's cock o'clock. *(The boys whoop with joy.)*

DIMITRI. Bring on the ladyfun. *(Harry answers the phone, motioning to the others to hush.)*

HARRY. Hello? Hi — are you here?

51

ED. Tell her I've got my cock out ready for her.

HARRY. He what? Oh fuck.

DIMITRI. What's happening?

HARRY. Landlord won't let her in.

GUY. What?

TOBY. Fucksticks.

ALISTAIR. Yeah, this is what I'm —

HARRY. Where are you now? *(Harry goes to the window and looks out.)* OK, go round to the left — no, we're in a room round the back. No no, he won't know —

JAMES. Is this a good idea?

HARRY. Can you see me at the window — I'm waving at you — OK, yeah, come here — *(Harry opens the window.)*

TOBY. You going out?

HARRY. No, she's coming in. *(Leans out of the window.)* Hi! *(A woman's face appears at the window.)*

CHARLIE. Hi. Harry?

HARRY. Charlie, yeah? *(Charlie looks into the room and sees all the other boys.)* This is Charlie, chaps, she's a — what d'you say, "call girl"?

CHARLIE. Um. Escort. Is this a stag party?

HARRY. No no, god no. Come in.

CHARLIE. Um. Might have to give me a hand.

HARRY. Pleasure. Is there a step on that —

CHARLIE. Yeah yeah. *(Harry gives Charlie his hand and she steps up to the window and swings one of her legs into the room.)* Dignified, isn't it?

HARRY. Spot of bother in the bar?

CHARLIE. Old client of mine's sat in there, tipped off the landlord. Usually meet somewhere a bit more discreet. *(Charlie brings her other leg through the window and faces the boys. She's wearing a demure(ish) black dress and heels. You'd have to be a seasoned punter to spot she was an escort.)*

HARRY. OK, well you're here now, so — This is my friends — James —

CHARLIE. Hi.

JAMES. Welcome. *(Charlie shakes James' hand, to the boys' surprise. She shakes hands with each of them as she's introduced.)*

HARRY. Alistair —

ALISTAIR. Hi.

HARRY. George — *(George giggles.)*

CHARLIE. Hello.

HARRY. Dimitri —

DIMITRI. Charmed.

HARRY. Guy, Toby — we call him Tubes —

CHARLIE. I won't ask why.

HARRY. Ed — he'll probably dribble on you —

CHARLIE. Ahh.

HARRY. Miles —

MILES. Hi.

HARRY. Oh and Hugo, but he's gay, so —

CHARLIE. Shame — you look like a catch.

HUGO. Thanks.

CHARLIE. *(Looks at Harry.)* So, um —

HARRY. Yeah. Here we are.

DIMITRI. Would you like a drink?

CHARLIE. Maybe in a minute, thanks. *(To Harry.)* You've got a room, have you?

HARRY. Yes. Here.

CHARLIE. *(Looks around at the room.)* This?

HARRY. Yeah.

CHARLIE. OK, where are the others going to go?

HARRY. Sorry?

CHARLIE. While we're seeing each other.

HARRY. No no, they'll be here. What we were thinking was if you, um, were under the table, and all of us sitting around it, so —

CHARLIE. What am I doing under the table?

HARRY. Um, us. One at a time.

DIMITRI. Slightly more than one at a time, maybe, um —

CHARLIE. You're talking about oral? On all of you.

MILES. We'd give you a cushion.

CHARLIE. What?

MILES. You know, for your knees.

HUGO. Milo —

CHARLIE. *(Laughs.)* Yeah, um. I'm sorry, there's been crossed lines here somewhere.

HARRY. Crossed lines?

CHARLIE. I do classic outcall — two hours, normal package. That's what I do. You seem to want more of a specialist thing.

GUY. What's the normal package?

CHARLIE. Straight sex or oral. Like a date, only I won't ring in the morning. Any extras have to be agreed in advance.

GUY. What counts as extras?

CHARLIE. Well, if you wanted BDSM or water sports or whatever, they'd send a girl who specialises. I do a more classy sort of service. Conversation. What did you say to the agency?

HARRY. Just said I wanted to hire a girl, I mean they didn't say —

CHARLIE. Did they not tell you extras had to be agreed in advance?

HARRY. Yeah, I just — I thought he was asking if I wanted more than one girl.

DIMITRI. Villiers.

HARRY. Well I don't know, they throw all these fucking euphemisms at you —

DIMITRI. One would probably assume we pay you and you do whatever's required.

CHARLIE. The agency should have made it clear —

HARRY. I've paid a deposit. Which I was given to believe is non-refundable.

CHARLIE. Yeah, you'll have to take that up with the agency.

DIMITRI. *(To Harry.)* You didn't think to check?

TOBY. Schoolboy, mate.

HARRY. Look, I'm sure we can work something out, can't we?

CHARLIE. What d'you mean?

HARRY. A considerably bigger fee? Which the agency needn't know about.

CHARLIE. I'm a professional.

HARRY. Yeah, course. Just it's an important night for us, and I —

CHARLIE. I don't do anything off the books.

HARRY. No, OK, but you're here now, so — These are special guys, Charlie, and we're celebrating tonight. I mean if you go away you don't earn the other half of the money, right?

CHARLIE. If you want to book a hotel room I'll happily go to it with you. *(James laughs.)*

HARRY. What, Leighton?

JAMES. We're not allowed to leave the room.

TOBY. There's no fucking point if we don't all get to do it.

HUGO. One for all and all for one.

ED. What if we *all* left the room in turn?

CHARLIE. I'm not going to do ten people in two hours.

HUGO. Make it nine.

CHARLIE. I don't do more than two visits in a row without a proper break.

HARRY. What break d'you need when you're just lying there? What?

CHARLIE. I'm not just a live version of the sock you wank into.

HARRY. OK, I'm not just a fucking wallet. Sorry, trying to be a gentleman here, but I'm actually really fucked off.

CHARLIE. You can take it up with Paul at the office if you want to complain.

HARRY. I do want to complain. I've been misled.

CHARLIE. Call him right now if you want.

HARRY. I will.

CHARLIE. You got the number?

HARRY. Yes thank you. *(Harry takes out his mobile and dials the number, putting the phone to his ear.)* Ringing.

HUGO. I know, why don't we leave it, try to keep a tiny scrap of dignity. *(George approaches Charlie.)*

GEORGE. 'Scuse me?

CHARLIE. Hi.

GEORGE. Don't you need the money?

CHARLIE. Not especially.

GEORGE. OK. You don't need some drugs, or —

TOBY. Balf —

CHARLIE. No I don't. Thank you.

GEORGE. So, why do you, um —

CHARLIE. I'm sorry?

GEORGE. Sorry, just wondering why you, you know —

CHARLIE. You want to finish that sentence?

GEORGE. No, I think I'll leave it.

JAMES. I'm never going to have an erection again.

HARRY. Fucking answerphone. *(Harry hangs up.)*

TOBY. Aren't you going to leave a message?

HARRY. And say what?

CHARLIE. Must be on the other line. You'll have to call him later.

DIMITRI. You don't think he'll be pissed off at you for losing a job?

CHARLIE. I don't have to do anything I don't want to. If I'm not one hundred per cent happy I can walk away.

HARRY. Look. Charlie. Here's my problem. I've promised these boys they'll get a blowjob tonight — if you don't do it, I look like a cunt.

CHARLIE. You could do it yourself — you'll be under the table, a mouth's a mouth.

HARRY. I'm not sure you quite appreciate who you're —

CHARLIE. I don't care who you are, it's —

HARRY. Why can't you just do it?

55

CHARLIE. I think I've made it clear what I —

HARRY. Why can't you buckle down and —

CHARLIE. What?

HARRY. Fuck's sake you're a whore, aren't you? *(The word hangs in the air.)*

CHARLIE. Right. I think I'm going now, aren't I? Yeah.

JAMES. D'you think you could exit through the window? Only we don't want the landlord —

CHARLIE. Whatever. *(Charlie steps up onto the chair by the window.)*

HARRY. No wait, wait, look Charlie I'm sorry, I didn't mean — we can work something out so everyone's — *(Harry grabs Charlie by the arm.)*

CHARLIE. Hands off.

ALISTAIR. Mate, step away. Let it go. *(Harry lets go of Charlie's arm. She's about to start climbing out of the window when the door opens and Chris comes in.)*

CHRIS. You — Out, please.

CHARLIE. Yeah, I'm going, I'm going.

ALISTAIR. Mate, it's fine, she's gone.

CHRIS. This is a family restaurant.

CHARLIE. I'm going, aren't I?

JAMES. It's alright, she's going.

CHARLIE. *(To Miles.)* Hand, please.

CHRIS. I won't have it, I've asked you nicely — *(Miles gives her his hand to help her out of the window.)*

CHARLIE. Shut up, I'm fucking going, OK?

CHRIS. Yes, well I'll be a lot happier once you've gone.

CHARLIE. I've gone I've gone. Jesus. *(Charlie, having climbed out of the window, disappears across the car park. Chris looks at the boys.)*

DIMITRI. I'm so sorry, is there a problem?

CHRIS. Yes, actually. Yes. I'm sorry, but I'm trying to run a family restaurant here.

GEORGE. Gastropub.

JAMES. Listen, I just want to say —

CHRIS. Look, you might like that sort of thing, I find it extremely offensive. Some of the lads from the village wanted a strippergram in here last year and I wouldn't let them — Can't have one rule for them and another for you — notwithstanding that it's against the law, what she —

DIMITRI. We're friends, aren't we? Let's not get into the legality issue.

CHRIS. I think it's time you left, please. *(George, James, and Guy head towards Chris, turning up the charm.)*

GEORGE. Oh no, please, come on —

JAMES. Really, we're everso sorry, can't we —

GUY. Thing is, most of us went to boarding school, we're not very good at —

CHRIS. The Ruby Wedding table — who by the way are sat just the other side of that wall — is threatening to leave if I don't turf you out, can't take the noise anymore.

JAMES. I'm so sorry, we really didn't realise —

GUY. You know what boys are like —

DIMITRI. It's our AGM, you see, so —

CHRIS. I'd like you to leave. I don't want to get the police involved. *(The other boys scramble towards Chris, trying to help placate him. Alistair stays where he is.)*

HARRY. The police? Hang on, let's —

HUGO. I'm sure we don't need to bother the police with —

TOBY. Fucking grow a pair.

HUGO. Tubes —

GUY. Honestly, we're just idiots, so —

CHRIS. When it's upsetting my other customers —

ALISTAIR. How much is the bill? *(The others fall quiet.)*

CHRIS. Sorry?

ALISTAIR. How much is the bill for the Ruby Wedding?

CHRIS. What's that got to —

ALISTAIR. We're spending what tonight —

JAMES. Al —

ALISTAIR. We're spending what tonight?

JAMES. 'Bout three and a half grand.

ALISTAIR. Three and a half thousand pounds. And the Ruby Wedding bill comes to what — how many of them?

CHRIS. Eight, but that's not —

ALISTAIR. Eight people off the set menu, six bottles of wine, fifteen per cent tip, I mean we're talking a few hundred, aren't we? Aren't we? Surely the question is — Is which of these two parties can you least afford to lose?

JAMES. Ryle, don't —

ALISTAIR. Let the man speak.

CHRIS. It's not about the money, it's about goodwill, these are my customers —

ALISTAIR. Exactly — what kind of customers do you want: hundreds or thousands? *(Alistair pauses for a moment to let Chris think.)* I tell you what. What say we pay the bill for the Ruby Wedding table? Gesture of *goodwill. (Alistair turns to the others: "Who's got the money?")* Right, chaps? *(Dimitri reaches into his jacket pocket and pulls out a wad of cash.)*

DIMITRI. What was it, three hundred pounds? Four? *(Dimitri counts out the money.)*

ALISTAIR. Make it five.

DIMITRI. Bottle of champagne as well. *(Dimitri holds the money towards Chris.)*

ALISTAIR. We might not be to your *taste*, but we always pay our way. *(Chris looks at the money.)* We wouldn't want you to be out of pocket. *(Chris takes the money.)*

CHRIS. Well. I'll see if they're happy with that.

ALISTAIR. Please do.

CHRIS. This is what they teach you at boarding school, is it?

ALISTAIR. Do send them our congratulations. *(Chris moves towards the door. James and Guy follow him.)*

JAMES. I'm very sorry — we're very sorry.

GUY. You see we don't get together very often, so when we see each other we get a bit over-excited.

TOBY. What about pudding?

ED. Yay pudding!

ALISTAIR. Send the girl in with the pudding. We'll be fine.

JAMES. The food's been excellent. Really.

GUY. Friends again, yes?

CHRIS. Just keep it down, please.

JAMES. You won't hear another squeak out of us, really.

GEORGE. Thank you!

CHRIS. Desserts'll be along in a minute. *Gentlemen. (Chris leaves. James closes the door.)*

ALISTAIR. What a fucking. Knob-jockey. *(All eyes turn to Alistair.)*

JAMES. Mate — he'll —

ALISTAIR. I don't care if he hears me.

DIMITRI. Fucking liberty.

ALISTAIR. You see what I mean?

JAMES. Come on, Al, he was —

ALISTAIR. Taking the piss, mate.

TOBY. Taking the fucking piss.

HUGO. "Is this what they teach you at boarding school?"

JAMES. We did try to get a prozzer through a — didn't chuck us out, did he? At least he was willing to —

ALISTAIR. Snide remarks with one hand, but he's still taking the money with the other, isn't he? Still taking the fucking money.

HARRY. "I'll see if they're happy with that."

ED. *Total* dickwad.

JAMES. You offered him a deal, he took it, what's the —

ALISTAIR. Yeah, but he keeps the moral high ground. 'Cause god forbid he gives that up. What about *not* take the money if you feel that fucking strongly? Or what about take the money and shut the fuck up?

TOBY. As if.

ALISTAIR. I mean who the fuck does he — Does he think he's some kind of *lord* 'cause he's got a gastropub? What, thin beef and gay puddings for people who think 'cause they're eating orange fish it must be smoked salmon?

HARRY. Gaylord.

ALISTAIR. Calling us "gentlemen" as if he had any *idea*, any idea of what the word means. Graciously letting us stay if we don't smoke or call a prozzer or make any noise — what is this, the fucking Quiet Carriage?

TOBY. Yeah! I mean *boo*.

ALISTAIR. I mean just 'cause he's got Farrow and Ball on the — what colour is that, *kidney*? — he reckons it gives him the right to sneer at us 'cause he's what, honest, decent, hardworking? He thinks he's earned it. He also thinks Rugby League is a sport. I mean this man keeps cheese in the fucking *fridge*.

HUGO. Which he should hang for, frankly.

ALISTAIR. "While you're under my roof you respect my rules"? I've got a new rule for you, mate, it's called survival of the fittest, it's called "Fuck you — we're the Riot Club." Respect that. "Can't have one rule for them and another rule for you" — Why not? Seriously, why the fuck not? We're the fucking Riot Club. And we've hardly started, mate. And *her*, stuck up bitch, fucking skank — you're a prostitute, love, get on your knees. "Not doing that, it's not in my job description," "I'm a professional, ring my line manager" — I'll wring your fucking neck if you're not careful. What, you're too good for us? We've got the finest sperm in the country in this room, she should be paying *us* to let her drink it.

HARRY. Fuck yeah. Girls queuing round the block.

ALISTAIR. And these people think *we're* twats. Are we going to sit here and take it, carry on taking it? Tonight of all nights?

GUY. The pâté tasted like jizz. There, I've said it.

HARRY. It fucking did.

ALISTAIR. This bourgeois outrage when we do anything, say *anything*. Lurking round every corner, trying to smoke us out. Anything we ever build or achieve, anything with the slightest whiff of magnificence — who the fuck are these people? How did they get *everywhere*, how did they make everything so fucking second-rate? Thinking they're cultured 'cause they read a big newspaper and eat asparagus and pretend not to be racist. Bursting a vein at the thought there's another floor their lift doesn't go up to, for all their *striving*. Honest, decent people hell-bent on turning this country to fuck. "You're not allowed to do that," "You can't have that, that's not fair." You know what's not fair? That we have to even listen to them. Thinking 'cause there's more of them they're better, when they're worth their weight in shit — that's not sweat on their palms, it's *envy*, it's resentment and it stinks like a fucking *drain* — I mean I am sick, I am sick to fucking death of *poor people*.

End of Act One

ACT TWO

Scene 1

The boys are eating pudding, faces close to large dishes of Eton mess.

ED. So my mother and father are stuck in this tiny little sitting room upstairs, huddled round a gas fire, rooms all round them getting opened to visitors 'cause they've got some cunting tapestry or William of Orange slept there. Next time I go back they'll have stuck my parents in the fucking buttery.

HARRY. Same at mine, mate.

ED. Held to ransom by the National Trust.

HARRY. Board of Trustees.

ED. Guides walking through the house saying "We restored this room last year," as if it's *theirs*.

ALISTAIR. Shameful.

HARRY. Last time I was home this guide woman — I think she must have been new — she told me I couldn't go behind one of the ropes. I said "Yes I can it's my house."

ED. Fucking sick of it.

TOBY. The *fucking. Wankers. (Toby drinks.)*

GEORGE. Haven't people always wanted a look inside big houses? We've always had visitors.

HUGO. They're not visitors now, they're *customers*.

HARRY. Every year it's thinking of new ways to get the punters in. Used to be just the summer, now they've got this German Christmas craft fair.

ED. Yeah, we're having that. Shitty wooden toys.

HARRY. Whole place smells of cinnamon.

ED. We're having husky races this year.

HARRY. And *endless* film crews, fucking Jane Austen.

HUGO. *Sex and Sexibility.*

ED. We've got to reschedule my sister's wedding because it clashes with the teddy bears' picnic and they've already done the leaflets. It's so *grubby*.

ALISTAIR. Yeah, exactly — we're all bending over backwards.

MILES. It's all about bears with you, isn't it?

HUGO. The age of compromise …

ED. It's an important collection.

JAMES. It's good, isn't it, if they want to visit? What history's for.

HUGO. No, because — no, Leighton, it's not *their* history. These are — these are private houses, family *homes*. And they were built by people who knew how to actually *live*, people with a bit of — I mean men who built things *big*, so big you look at them now and think god, how many people did that take to — And lived *unapologetically*, that's the thing. Defended themselves if they needed to, I mean they wrote the history of this country in their own *blood*. Built these houses as proof of their, their *magnificence* because they were proud of who they were and what they stood for. Now they're trampled through by people only there for the cream tea and the novelty thimble.

HARRY. Except they don't want the cream tea anymore, reckon the buns are "too expensive." Everything's about *value for money*, grubby little voucher schemes.

GUY. Fucking recession, isn't it?

ALISTAIR. Happening before the recession, mate. Blair's lot, giving the kids too much pocket money —

HARRY. "Because you're worth it."

DIMITRI. Yawn.

HUGO. *(Turning to James.)* Why should Ed's family have to put up with their house getting turned into a theme park?

JAMES. Because otherwise they couldn't afford to get the roof fixed.

GEORGE. Always the roof.

ED. Roof wouldn't be a problem if they hadn't taken all the money when grandpa died.

JAMES. Yeah, OK, but you know, your parents made a decision, didn't they, to open the —

GEORGE. Our roof's got holes you could fire a cow through.

DIMITRI. Bored of the roof now!

JAMES. I'm just saying your family benefited from —

HARRY. Yeah, till they stopped coming.

ALISTAIR. And we know why they stopped, don't we? 'Cause they spent all the money on all this shiny new shit — massive fuckoff plasma-screen telly. Don't understand why they're not just born with it, why it doesn't just get handed to them —

JAMES. OK, sure, "mistakes were made," but our lot are in power now, so —

GUY. True dat.

ALISTAIR. We're not in power.

GUY. They'll get a majority next time, my uncle says —

ALISTAIR. Does it *feel* like we're in power? Or does it feel like that fucking landlord, like people like him still get to shit wherever they want and we're just trailing round with a poop-scoop?

DIMITRI. Come on guys, who runs the world?

ALISTAIR. Not us. Clearly. These people have gashed it up for us. We're all going to come out of college —

HARRY. Which we worked fucking hard for, don't forget —

ALISTAIR. Yeah, and there's going to be no jobs for us because of people like him.

TOBY. I mean these people — *these people* —

JAMES. OK fine. Everyone's suffering.

ED. My brother's been made redundant.

HARRY. Monters?

JAMES. Where was he, Merrill?

ED. Goldman.

GEORGE. But your brother's a legend.

ED. Legend as in used to have a job, now doesn't.

DIMITRI. He was only there five minutes.

ED. Last in, first out, isn't it?

DIMITRI. Shit.

ED. No, I mean, he's *OK*. Says he going to buy an Airstream — one of those big old silver caravan things? Start a business doing street food at festivals and shit. You know, *really* good burgers? *(The boys think about this for a moment.)*

ALISTAIR. I mean, *fuck.*

GUY. The fucking landlord.

HARRY. We should totally do something to fuck him up.

TOBY. The trouble is, right, the trouble is that these people — they've got no fucking — I mean, have they? What a load of fucking — fuck it makes me angry —

JAMES. I just don't understand how you're pinning Monters' redundancy on the landlord of this pub.

HARRY. He took our prozzer away, we should get him back.

ALISTAIR. Not just *him*, people like him.

GUY. Get the daughter back in.

ALISTAIR. I mean, when you trace it back, yeah?

TOBY. What I mean is — 'scuse me — *(Toby starts to ramble incoherently, a few phrases audible here and there.)*

JAMES. Yeah, just a bit of a *hardline* position, isn't —

ALISTAIR. OK. Fuck. Let's join it up, shall we? So, OK, they want all the *stuff*, ninety-five per cent mortgage, whatever, so they all borrow more money than they can ever afford to pay back.

TOBY. And that cunt of a girl going all "Oh Toby" —

ALISTAIR. They're obsessed with upward mobility but they're not prepared to put the work in, it's all credit cards.

TOBY. And then I fucking said —

ALISTAIR. Then when the great New Labour shop in the sky goes up in flames 'cause it turns out there *isn't* an endless supply of toys and sweets, there can't be —

TOBY. … should have gone Christ Church …

ALISTAIR. They vote us back in to sort it all out, make it all go away.

JAMES. Yeah, OK, 'cause we're good at solving —

ALISTAIR. Haven't finished. But then they're all —

TOBY. Because I've got the *right*, right —

ALISTAIR. But then they're all like "Oh no, but don't do it like that," they don't —

TOBY. My *human rights* —

ALISTAIR. Fuck's sake, I'm trying to — someone put Tubes to bed, yeah?

ED. Yeah yeah. Mate?

TOBY. Hello.

ED. Alright mate — how about a little sleep? *(Toby bangs his fist on the table, nearly upsetting his pudding bowl.)*

TOBY. No sleeping at the table!

JAMES. Yeah, put him on the window seat or something.

ED. Come on, mate, let's go and have a sit by the window.

TOBY. OK. *(Ed leads Toby over to the window seat, Toby still muttering to himself.)*

ED. Nice bit of Bedfordshire.

ALISTAIR. So they call us in —

TOBY. The Duke of Bedfordshire! *(Toby stumbles and falls, stopping Alistair.)*

ALISTAIR. Jesus. *(Harry and Miles stand up to help Ed.)*

HARRY. That's it, mate.

ED. Come on, sleepy-byes, OK?

TOBY. OK. Love you. *(Harry and Miles get Toby to the window and help to settle him on the seat. George puts his hand up.)*

GEORGE. Uh, guys, while we're *paused* — does anyone not want their pudding? *(Toby puts his head down on the windowsill in front of him and goes to sleep.)*

GUY. Have Toby's one. *(Ed, Harry, and Miles make their way back to the table.)*

GEORGE. Super — chuck it over. *(The pudding is passed over to him.)* Yummy. Sorry Ryle, you were saying — there's a sweet shop —

ALISTAIR. No, they call us in to sort it out 'cause yes, we're good at that. But they don't want to give up the big house and the massive telly, 'cause now they've got used to the idea that they're worth it. It's an impossible job, they've fucked us in every hole so I mean in what sense are we in power, Leighton?

DIMITRI. OK, looking a lot like a conversation about politics here, can I just say?

GUY. State of the world, mate. Everything's political.

DIMITRI. I'm here for the wine and the jokes.

GUY. 'Cause you've got no heritage, that's why.

DIMITRI. I've got a boatload of —

GUY. No, mate, you've got a boat.

GEORGE. He's right, should be scrunching for talking about politics —

ALISTAIR. It's not your fault you can't see it, mate. People get used to being shat on, don't they?

JAMES. Oh come on, for fuck's sake — we're not being —

ALISTAIR. Seriously, mate. "Them and us" all over again.

GEORGE. No no no, it's not, it's not at all. It's not them and us. You know, at home, we're all suffering — my family, the people who work on the estate, the chaps in the village, in the pub, yeah? We've got a responsibility to help each other. And, you know, they look to people like us, to guide them, to —

ALISTAIR. They don't want to be *guided*.

GEORGE. Yes they do.

ALISTAIR. They don't like us.

GUY. They hate us.

GEORGE. I just had a very nice drink with —

ALISTAIR. Who bought the drinks?

GEORGE. Sorry?

ALISTAIR. Who paid for the drinks?

GEORGE. I did.

ALISTAIR. Yeah. You think Farmer Barleymow and his mates aren't laughing at you out there right now? Dr Doolittle could talk to the animals, it didn't mean they wanted to be mates with him. George, *they hate you. (George looks down at the table, takes a drink.)*

MILES. Haven't we just got to find a way to coexist? With people who are different. I mean when I was in Malawi, right, there were people who had nothing, literally nothing, and they didn't —

ALISTAIR. I'm not talking about proper poor people, like Africa or whatever.

DIMITRI. Bored of Africa!

HUGO. What about Brixton?

MILES. What? Shut up.

ALISTAIR. What's this?

MILES. It's got nothing to do with it.

HUGO. You had four stitches.

MILES. Mate —

HUGO. Miles got attacked. Brixton one night.

HARRY. What were you doing in Brixton?

MILES. Went to a gig. People get mugged, it doesn't mean —

HUGO. I don't think it was a group of disgruntled Wykehamists.

MILES. It wasn't 'cause of being —

HUGO. What, you think they can't tell? You think you *blend in*? It's not like they're trying to coexist with us, is it?

GUY. How did it all get so shit?

ED. The bloody landlord!

ALISTAIR. No, mate. It's us. We let it happen.

ED. Did we?

ALISTAIR. We apologised. We *apologise* for being who we are, appropriate their values, pretend we agree with their fucking prudish — Like Leighton, hanging out the back of that landlord all night — "I'm so everso sorry" —

GUY. Yeah, "You won't hear another squeak out of us."

JAMES. Mate —

ALISTAIR. We do it to ourselves, yeah — all this shit about respecting other people's cultures — what, nicking trainers 'cause you can't be arsed to get a job and then calling it legitimate social protest? Fuck off. How about you respect *my* culture?

JAMES. Well, OK, because —

ALISTAIR. 'Cause it's only going to get worse. More discontent, more *legitimate* protest.

DIMITRI. Fuck, can somebody pass me that sword so I can stab my ears off? Yeah fine, the country's gone to shit — d'you know what I think we should do? Get out of town for the night, get wasted. *(Dimitri stands up.)* Have a look under your placemats, chaps — little something for each of you. *(The boys lift up their placemats and pull out an unfamiliar-looking bank note, which they examine.)* You know, what's this club *for*? What are we doing getting all misty about how hard done by we are? Let's fuck off somewhere, take copious party drugs, drink ourselves to oblivion, and raise merry hell.

MILES. One thousand. *(Reading.) Eitt Pusund Krónur.*

GUY. Eat poos and what?

DIMITRI. Icelandic. We're going to Reykjavik.

ALISTAIR. Iceland.

DIMITRI. Gather ye rosebuds, mate.

ED. Reykjavik.

GUY. What are we doing, fiscal irresponsibility tour?

DIMITRI. It's an all-night party city. I've been.

ALISTAIR. Persuade them into the euro?

JAMES. We're going tonight?

DIMITRI. Yes, come on! One thousand krónur — that's about a fiver in Icelandic money — not very much, but take it as a provocation, see how many vodkas you can get for it. And this — *(He pulls out a wad of English money and flamboyantly attaches it to the table with Lord Riot's sabre.)* Is for the first man to piss on an ice sculpture. *(Silence.)*

GEORGE. Wouldn't that just make it melt?

DIMITRI. Chaps, what's wrong with you? Come on.

GUY. I don't know, mate. All looks a bit flashy.

DIMITRI. Predictable response from Bell-end.

ALISTAIR. D'you really think that'll solve it?

DIMITRI. I'm not being —

HUGO. Waving money about again, Dims.

GUY. All he's got left, isn't it?

HUGO. Fiddling while Athens burns.

GUY. 'Cause he hasn't got a country anymore, so —

DIMITRI. I'm a British Citizen.

GUY. Wearing a cravat doesn't make you British, mate. This Mr Toad shit — who the fuck are you fooling?

DIMITRI. Fuck you, Bellingfield. Come on, chaps. *(Toby emits a strangled moan and twitches slightly.)*

TOBY. Wuuuugh. *(The others notice but carry on.)*

ALISTAIR. Dims, the trouble with going to Iceland is we'd have to come back. *(Another noise from Toby, whose body suddenly twitches and writhes.)*

TOBY. Mnnnnngh …

ALISTAIR. Fuck's sake, Tubes.

HUGO. You OK, Maitland?

GEORGE. Better out than in, mate. *(Toby stands up and staggers backwards into the room, still facing the window.)*

MILES. Whoa, careful mate —

HUGO. Tubes, what you — *(Toby turns around to face the boys. But it's not Toby anymore. The boys sit up in fright. Toby appears to have morphed into an eighteenth-century libertine. His voice comes out a little strangled at first, but commanding.)*

LORD RIOT. Gentlemen! *(He looks around at the boys. Those at the end of the table nearest to him make a dash for the other end, cowering behind James.)* Gentlemen of the Riot Club! Why suffer ye this plague of peasants? Ye stand there wronged yet unequal to a fight — where are your wigs, men?

ED. Where the fuck is Toby?

JAMES. Maitland, stop being a —

HUGO. Mate, look at him — *it's not Maitland.*

DIMITRI. What the fuck?

HUGO. I think it's Lord Riot.

GUY. I think we're supposed to speak to it.

LORD RIOT. *It?*

GUY. Him, sorry, him.

JAMES. Hugo?

HUGO. Why me?

GEORGE. He might do verse.

HUGO. Right, alright. Um. Are you. Lord Riot?

LORD RIOT. Ye should know me by now.

HUGO. No, yes, of course. My lord.

LORD RIOT. What appalling inaction is this? I find ye sitting like ladies at a bun shop, consumed by petty skirmishes.

HUGO. Yes. Yes, sorry about that.

LORD RIOT. Do not weep into your syllabub, boys, with tales of how the world has bruised you. Is this the purpose for which my club was founded? A licking of wounds?

HUGO. No, um, probably —

LORD RIOT. Leave off *quacking* and listen.

HUGO. Right. Sorry.

LORD RIOT. I have been at every dinner since the club's inception, whether or not my presence was remarked. Rarely have I had great enough cause to intervene and it pains me to do so now, but intervene I must.

JAMES. Um, should we be sitting down?

LORD RIOT. Why must you brawl among yourselves? Ye are the finest of men, of all men — your fight is not with each other. I know you feel your country running away from you, intent on mediocrity, garbling every morsel of magnificence into an inglorious gruel. But we have seen worse, boys, we have seen worse, and without *whining*. When our French cousins were guillotined, did *we* weep into our pudding or did we stand our ground? Under your last queen, when legions of oily industrialists built machines they thought would make us obsolete, did we not show them *our* mettle? Ninety years since, when the common man downed tools in peevish discontent, your counterparts stepped into the breach, uncomplaining. Drove omnibuses! Succeeded in putting the country back on its feet in but nine days. The landlords of this world have thrown every kind of ordure at us down the years — are we not *still here*? Do you think I would let these merchants and hustlers quench my every fire with scorn and outrage? Are they the masters now, and you the servants? Aye, boys, your times are bleak, but let them not divide you. You are the brightest, the boldest, the best. You think the true purpose of the club is simply the making of merriment? A place in which you *hide*? Never! The world wants you, boys — though it may not yet know it — it wants you, and it wants you to *lead*.

ALISTAIR. OK, so what should we do?

LORD RIOT. If you do not like what they have built, tear it down. Where is your wit, where is your imagination? Tear it down and build something better — they will thank you in the end.

ALISTAIR. Right, so how do we — *(There's a knock at the door, at which Lord Riot freezes, then droops, deflates.)*

HUGO. Shit. *(The door opens a crack.)*

ALISTAIR. Wait! *(The boys cluster around Lord Riot. Rachel comes in.)*

HARRY. Shit — fuck —

ALISTAIR. I said wait — *(The boys try to hide Lord Riot behind them, masking Rachel's view.)*

HARRY. Rachel! Why-eye!

RACHEL. Um. Yes. Howay the lads. Sorry, I need to clear the —

JAMES. Yes, lovely, thank you.

RACHEL. What have you — Who've you got —

HARRY. Who've we what?

JAMES. *(Gestures to the table.)* Please, go ahead and —

RACHEL. Have you got someone behind —

JAMES. What? No, nothing —

RACHEL. You've got that woman, haven't you, look, you can't bring a — *(Rachel heads confidently towards the cluster of boys.)*

HARRY. No no no, it's —

TOBY. Wuugh the fuck are you — *(On hearing Toby's voice, the boys move back from him, in relief.)*

HARRY. No, it's just Toby, see.

ED. Toby!

JAMES. Fuck, thank fuck.

TOBY. Did you just touch my jonty?

ALISTAIR. *(To Rachel.)* Just Toby, look.

RACHEL. Right. Sorry, I thought —

DIMITRI. Tubes, mate — you alright?

TOBY. Fuck I'm gunna chunder … No I'm not.

GUY. OK, have a sit down, mate. *(They lead Toby to sit down in the nearest chair.)*

RACHEL. What's wrong with him?

TOBY. My mouth tastes like —

ED. Just a bit tired. Lots of essays.

TOBY. Did I eat a *fox*?

JAMES. Tuck him in, yeah. *(To Rachel.)* Please, go ahead and clear. *(Alistair and Harry tuck Toby's chair closer into the table and he puts his head down on his hands. Rachel puts her tray on a small service table at the side of the room, then moves to the table to start collecting the pudding dishes.)*

ALISTAIR. *(To Harry.)* Mate, what about — *(Alistair nods towards Rachel. Harry nods back, understanding.)*

HARRY. Yeah, cool.

GUY. Rachel, can I just say that was the messiest Eton mess I ever had. And I went to Eton.

RACHEL. Good.

ALISTAIR. Rachel?

RACHEL. Hi.

ALISTAIR. Hi. How'd you like to earn an extra £300 tonight?

RACHEL. What? *(Alistair and Harry laugh. The laugh passes around the table as the other boys cotton on.)*

ALISTAIR. OK, here's what the thing is — we had this friend, this lady friend — well, as you know — who was supposed to be here with us right now, but actually — whoops — your dad's sent her away, so —

RACHEL. Right.

ALISTAIR. So we wondered if you might like to step in.

ED. Oh my god, did he just ask that?

RACHEL. Me?

ALISTAIR. Pretty easy way to make £300.

RACHEL. Are you asking what I think you're asking?

ALISTAIR. No! God no. Only blowjobs.

GUY. Under the table.

ED. Yeah, you'd be under the table so you wouldn't have to see who you're —

MILES. Head-down Harriet.

ED. Subtable Susan.

ALISTAIR. Simple transaction — professional basis.

RACHEL. I'll leave it, thank you.

ALISTAIR. No, fine. Very modern. *(Alistair laughs.)*

MILES. We're just joking, Rachel.

RACHEL. OK.

ED. Don't be offended, it's just jokes, yeah?

ALISTAIR. Just a bit over-excited.

RACHEL. Right, OK.

HARRY. I'm sorry, Rachel.

RACHEL. OK.

ED. Sorry. *(They subside a little. Harry and Alistair look at each other. Harry bangs his hand on the table.)*

HARRY. Chelsea Trots!

GEORGE. Hurrah.

DIMITRI. Fuck's sake.

HARRY. *(To Dimitri.)* Mate — forfeits, yeah?

ED. What?

HARRY. *(Pointing at Rachel.)* Forfeits.

ED. Oh OK, yeah.

ALISTAIR. Places! *(The boys start to move into place, spreading out around the table. Alistair looks at Miles. Miles looks at Rachel.)*

MILES. D'you um, want to play, Rachel?

HARRY. Quick game of the Chelsea Trots?

RACHEL. I don't know what that is.

GUY. You must do, everyone does. *(The boys move the chairs back from the table to give them more room.)*

HARRY. Balf — you explain it to Rachel, yeah? George is from a long line of champion Trotters.

GEORGE. Basically what happens is everyone dances round the circle and when the music stops you sit down, only there's one chair too few, so —

RACHEL. Musical Chairs.

GEORGE. If you like.

GUY. We playing Banbury Rules or Standard?

ALISTAIR. Banbury, I think. Balf?

GEORGE. Yeah, Banbury. So you go round, right, and when the music stops —

RACHEL. What are you going to play the music on?

GEORGE. Sorry?

RACHEL. Did you ask for a CD player?

GEORGE. Oh no, there's isn't any music.

RACHEL. You said "When the music stops."

GEORGE. Yeah, you just know when it stops.

GUY. It's usually quite obvious.

RACHEL. I think I'll sit this one out. *(The boys roll the bottom of their trousers up.)*

ALISTAIR. Oh boo. Really?

HARRY. OK, you'll have to just go round Rachel, OK, 'cause she's still clearing, so when you get to her, just go right round, like this, OK?

ALISTAIR. Ready?

HUGO. Chair! *(They move one chair so it's against the wall by the door. They all stand ready, facing clockwise. Alistair looks at Rachel.)*

ALISTAIR. Here we go. *(A look goes round the group, with coded gestures pointing at Rachel.)*

GEORGE. Wait for it — Standpipe! *(Ed nearly starts going round, then stops.)* Think about it … Bandicoot! *(For some reason this is the right word, and the boys start to dance around the circle, wild and exuberant. Rachel continues to try to clear the plates from the table, trying not to look at the boys and laugh. Each time one of them gets to her he makes a big thing of going around her.)*

JAMES. New boys should be going in the opposite direction.

MILES. OK. *(Miles turns and dances in the opposite direction. Ed is already doing so. To Ed.)* You played this at school, right?

ED. Yeah, didn't you?

DIMITRI. This is so much better after a sniffy. *(Exactly in unison, the boys suddenly all stop dancing and make a dash for the nearest chair. James is the only one who doesn't find a chair in time.)*

GUY. Forfeit Leighton!

JAMES. OK, and my forfeit is —

GEORGE. President can't decide his own forfeit.

JAMES. Ryle, you want to nominate?

ALISTAIR. OK, your forfeit, should you choose to accept it —

HARRY. You have to accept it.

ALISTAIR. Is to drink a bottle down in one!

JAMES. *(Glances at Rachel.)* What, don't I get — I thought we were doing —

ALISTAIR. Warm-up round.

JAMES. Fuck, OK.

HARRY. Bottle for Leighton-Masters. *(James climbs onto a chair and a full bottle of wine is handed to him. He drinks half of it while the others cheer, but has to stop and take a breath. He staggers. Even Rachel stops her clearing-up to watch.)*

ALISTAIR. Come on, Leighton.

GEORGE. Don't give up, mate, come on. *(He downs the rest of the bottle and looks very much as if he'll vomit on the spot, but in fact doesn't. He holds the bottle high and the boys cheer.)* Off we go! *(The boys dance around the circle, as before, and at the same moment, all dash for chairs. This time it's Miles who doesn't get one.)*

MILES. Ah, bollocks.

GEORGE. And it's Mr Miley Milo Richards for the forfeit.

HARRY. Take it like a man, Milo.

GEORGE. Forfeit, Ryle?

ALISTAIR. Aaaand, your forfeit is … You have to kiss Rachel.

RACHEL. What? No no.

HUGO. You can't do sexual forfeits.

ALISTAIR. Forfeits are freestyle. Banbury Rules. *(Rachel makes for the door with a pile of dishes in her hand.)*

HARRY. No no no, don't go. Don't go.

RACHEL. I've got to get back to the kitchen.

GUY. Play the game, Rachel.

RACHEL. I said I'm not playing. *(Someone takes the pile of dishes from her. Rachel is edged back into the room, away from the door.)*

ALISTAIR. If you're in the room, you're playing the game.

HARRY. Just a kiss.

RACHEL. I don't want to.

HUGO. Don't make him —

GUY. What, is it not in your job description?

DIMITRI. You can't turn down a forfeit, Rachel, it's disrespectful to our culture.

ED. We'll feel disrespected.

HUGO. Don't make Milo kiss her, come on.

RACHEL. Sorry, I'm not —

DIMITRI. What about a blowjob, then?

RACHEL. No way. *(The boys laugh.)*

DIMITRI. Rachel. The man's a thoroughbred.

GUY. Best sperm in the country — you should be thanking us.

DIMITRI. Just have to kneel down and shut your eyes.

ALISTAIR. Guys, guys, she doesn't have to give him a blojo. *(Rachel makes a move towards the door.)* You just have to kiss him.

MILES. Wait, Rachel, Rachel. Don't you want to, even a bit? Come on.

HUGO. Miles —

RACHEL. No, I. No.

ALISTAIR. Have you got a boyfriend, Rachel, is that it?

RACHEL. Yes. Actually.

ALISTAIR. Nice, is he?

RACHEL. Yes. He is.

ALISTAIR. Treats you nice. Takes you out — cinema, nice Italian —

DIMITRI. Probably splits the bill.

ALISTAIR. D'you split the bill, Rachel? Bet you split the bill. You telling me you wouldn't trade up if you had the chance? *(Miles steps forward and without warning grabs Rachel and kisses her on the mouth. He holds her firmly in his arms so that she struggles, but can't get free of him. Eventually Rachel manages to pull away, and turns to try to get to the door, but there are too many boys in the way for her to push through.)*

HUGO. Let her out.

RACHEL. Let me out.

HARRY. Didn't you like it? *(A strangled noise comes from Toby. He sits up, his body heaving. The others notice at once.)*

ED. Tubes?

GUY. Fuck, is he going again? *(The others gather around him, concerned, clearing the way to the door.)*

TOBY. No, fine, I'm fine. *(Rachel dashes out. Harry notices and takes a step towards the door, but Alistair stops him.)*

ALISTAIR. Let her go — bigger fish, yeah?

ED. Chaps, don't crowd him. *(Toby runs his hands through his hair, knocking the wig off without realising.)*

HUGO. *(To Miles.)* What the fuck was that?

MILES. I'm not your rent boy.

HUGO. Yeah, I got that.

TOBY. *(He looks around.)* Are we still being sad?

ALISTAIR. No, mate — we're just getting going.

TOBY. Awesome. I am the Trashmeister.

ALISTAIR. Let's do this!

ED. You want to give the pins a go, mate? *(Toby stands up — he's a little wobbly, then regains his balance.)*

TOBY. Whoa — there we go. Back in the snaddle.

HARRY. Sabrage!

ALISTAIR. Erect the barricade! *(Dimitri grabs a chair and puts it under the door handle.)*

GUY. Quick — quick — get the champagne.

DIMITRI. Barricade erect, my lord.

GEORGE. God I love this. *(Alistair climbs up to stand on the table.)*

GUY. Champagne!

ALISTAIR. Everyone feeling frisky? *(A bottle of champagne is handed to Alistair.)* And the sword.

GUY. Sword! *(Harry hands Alistair the sabre.)*

ALISTAIR. Never let it be said we don't take our work seriously, chaps. *(Alistair turns to James, holding the champagne and the sabre towards him.)* Sorry, should you be —

JAMES. No mate, you do it.

ALISTAIR. Gentlemen — for what we're about to do, may the good Lord Riot make us truly trashful. Let's make this one extra spicy. *(Alistair holds the champagne in front of him, swiping the sword along the neck of the bottle.)*

ALL. HO! *(The cork flies off and champagne sprays everywhere. The club roars. They set to work trashing the room: it's orchestrated and rhythmic, almost balletic. It goes on for ages. Crockery is smashed, plants overturned, pictures pulled down from the wall and headbutted or drop-kicked out of their frames, wallpaper torn, chairs pulled apart, a plant pot thrown through a window pane ... They continue until a banging on the door is heard. It might have been going on for some time.)*

CHRIS. If you don't open this door, I'm going to have to —

MILES. Shit, guys — the landlord.

ALISTAIR. Leave him, door's safe. We'll let him in when we're — *(The door flies open and Chris is propelled into the room.)* For fuck's sake! Who did the barricade?

CHRIS. *(Looks around.)* Oh my g — Oh Jesus what have you — What have you — *(Toby giggles, high-pitched.)* What the hell do you think you're playing at?

ALISTAIR. Get him out, we're not finished.

GUY. You know what boys are like. *(Chris sees the smashed window.)*

CHRIS. You've broken the —

ALISTAIR. We said before we'd pay our way. You won't be out of pocket — show him the money. *(Dimitri comes towards Chris holding a wad of cash.)*

CHRIS. *(To Dimitri, pointing at Alistair.)* I want to talk to him.

DIMITRI. OK, this is —

CHRIS. I don't want your money.

DIMITRI. We made a deal.

CHRIS. I didn't make any deal.

DIMITRI. Four hundred pounds? Earlier?

ALISTAIR. Five hundred.

DIMITRI. Sorry, five hundred. D'you remember?

CHRIS. That wasn't a deal.

DIMITRI. I think there's a misunderstanding — we all saw you take the money,

CHRIS. Just for that one party.

JAMES. Sorry, we thought you'd understood.

ALISTAIR. For fuck's sake.

CHRIS. Don't start with me, my friend.

JAMES. Look, here's what —

CHRIS. *(To Alistair.)* You — What the hell d'you think gives you the right —

ALISTAIR. You want to persist in being stupid? Sit down.

CHRIS. I won't sit —

ALISTAIR. Sit. Down. Sit him down. *(Harry and Dimitri pick up a chair and lead Chris backwards to sit on it.)*

GEORGE. Chaps. Let's all be — let's be gentlemen, shall we?

CHRIS. Gentlemen.

ALISTAIR. *(To Chris.)* Shut up and listen. This is what happens. You go back out there quietly and we do this and we pay you. We pay you a large amount of money — in cash — an amount of money that will well and truly cover the costs of your repairs, with

76

something left over, most likely — which, by the way, is more than you'd ever get out of an insurance company. We pay you and we go away and everyone's happy. Alright?

CHRIS. "Everyone's happy"? What you've done to my pub —

ALISTAIR. Fuck's sake. *(Alistair takes the wad of cash from Dimitri.)* This. Is for you. OK? Whatever repairs you need, and plenty left over to take your daughter to Bicester Village, nice pair of shoes.

CHRIS. She doesn't want your money either. *(Alistair holds the cash close to Chris's face. He looks at it.)*

ALISTAIR. Those are fifties, in case that helps the mental arithmetic you're doing right now.

DIMITRI. We know how much it costs to do up a place like this, we've got experience.

CHRIS. People let you do this?

ALISTAIR. If you're smart you'll take the treats and shut up. *(Alistair puts the wad of cash in Chris's lap. Chris looks at it then brushes it off onto the floor.)*

CHRIS. I don't want your money.

ALISTAIR. Don't push me.

GEORGE. OK, guys, let's —

CHRIS. I don't want your money.

ALISTAIR. Yes you do. *(Chris goes to stand up, but Alistair advances with menace, and he sits again.)* Yes you fucking do. It's the only reason we're still here, 'cause you know there's a fistful of notes coming at the end of the night.

CHRIS. Think you can buy your way out of anything, don't you? People like you think the world —

ALISTAIR. Oh I know, you're torn up inside cause you think you don't like me. News for you, guv — you fucking love me, you'd like to *be* me but you can't quite admit it, can you? Chip on your shoulder much? I mean what are you trying to do with this tawdry little cunt-shack? Private dining? What the fuck? Walking round like you own the place — but hang on, technically the *bank* owns the place, doesn't it? Have you paid off the loan for the conversion? No, thought not. *(Re: the money.)* This would do it, wouldn't it? Now why don't you fuck off and let us finish the job? *(Miles and Ed have collected up the money from the floor, and put it back on Chris's lap.)*

CHRIS. Something happened to my daughter in here.

ALISTAIR. Your daughter? What?

CHRIS. Very funny look on her face when she walked out of here a few minutes ago. Said you were playing silly buggers — some kind of kiss-chase thing, "Nothing to worry about, Dad," but who's to say it wasn't more than that? 'Cause if someone touched her inappropriately —

HARRY. What are you alleging?

CHRIS. I'm saying maybe you assaulted my daughter.

ALISTAIR. *Assaulted* her?

CHRIS. Ten of you in the room, innocent young girl?

TOBY. No one fucking assaulted your daughter.

CHRIS. I heard you, muttering obscenities earlier.

TOBY. Me? What obscenities?

CHRIS. Something about "pussy."

TOBY. Fuck's sake.

CHRIS. If any of you so much as tapped her on the shoulder —

ALISTAIR. Mate, we wouldn't touch her with a bargepole.

TOBY. Wouldn't fuck her with a bargepole.

CHRIS. You what?

ALISTAIR. He said your daughter's a fucking slapper. I've got a room full of guys who saw her flashing herself about, total prick tease. You don't wear a black bra under a white shirt without meaning something.

CHRIS. You want a sexual assault conviction, the lot of you?

DIMITRI. Sorry — *what?*

CHRIS. Follow you around your whole life, that will.

TOBY. The fuck are you saying?

CHRIS. 'Cause that's not something you can pay your way out of. *(Alistair boils over, suddenly aims a swift uppercut at Chris's chin. It comes from somewhere deep and horrible. Chris stands — it's unclear if he's trying to escape or fight back. Guy, Harry and Miles all throw themselves at him, kicking and punching with fervour. Toby lunges in, too. They stop when Chris falls to the floor, unconscious. Toby continues to kick him as the others stop, horrified, looking at what they've done.)*

GEORGE. Toby. Toby. *(Toby desists and takes a step back. The boys go quiet, looking at Chris. Is he dead?)*

HUGO. Fuck. Guys? *(Dimitri goes towards Chris's prone body.)*

GUY. Is he OK?

JAMES. *(To Alistair.)* What the fuck are you doing?

TOBY. Oops.

ALISTAIR. He pushed me.

JAMES. Is he breathing?

DIMITRI. I don't know yet.

JAMES. Jesus. *(Ed starts to cry.)*

DIMITRI. I don't know, does anyone know first aid?

HUGO. First aid? Need a fucking ambulance.

GEORGE. Find a pulse. *(George kneels down and listens next to Chris's mouth.)*

ED. What have you done?

TOBY. Shut up.

JAMES. What if he dies?

ALISTAIR. He's not going to —

JAMES. He might. You beat the living shit out of him.

ALISTAIR. He fucking pushed me.

DIMITRI. OK, he's got a pulse.

MILES. Thank fuck.

DIMITRI. Pretty faint, though. *(Hugo takes out his phone.)*

HUGO. I'm going to call an ambulance.

MILES. Mate, please.

TOBY. My dad is going to —

ALISTAIR. Hugo, don't call a — *(Miles goes towards Hugo, as if to snatch the phone, but Hugo steps back, holding up his hand.)*

HUGO. Don't —

ALISTAIR. Shit.

HUGO. *(Into phone.)* Ambulance, please.

TOBY. Fucking hell.

DIMITRI. Hang up hang up.

HUGO. *(Into phone.)* Yeah, the um, Bull's Head Inn, Kidsbury. Um, sort of a *disturbance*.

ED. I want to go home.

ALISTAIR. Man up, Eddie.

HUGO. Someone's unconscious —

DIMITRI. Say he fell.

HUGO. Yeah, he — he fell — How what? How did he fall? *(Hugo looks at Alistair.)* He got punched.

GUY. Fuck's sake, Tyrwhitt.

HUGO. No, it's um — fight's over.

TOBY. Mate, seriously — *(Hugo looks at Chris.)*

HUGO. I don't know, forties. I don't know him. He's the landlord. Yeah, he's unconscious now.

DIMITRI. Give me the phone.

HUGO. OK. Yeah. Let me just —

ALISTAIR. Give him the fucking —

DIMITRI. Give me the phone.

HUGO. Fuck off! *(Into phone.)* No, not you. *(Hugo kneels down, checking if Chris is breathing.)* Yeah, he is. Yeah. Yeah. Thank you. *(To the others.)* On its way. *(Into phone.)* Yeah, I'll stay on the line, OK.

ED. Oh my god oh my god. *(Dimitri grabs Hugo's phone and hangs up.)*

HUGO. She told me to —

DIMITRI. Got to work out what we're going to say.

ALISTAIR. Jesus, why the fuck did you have to —

HUGO. Ten of us in the room and none of us gets an ambulance, how does that look?

DIMITRI. Should have talked about it first —

HUGO. And then maybe he dies while we're discussing —

DIMITRI. They'll send the fucking police, mate — you told them there's been a fight.

HUGO. Fuck.

ALISTAIR. Yeah, fuck. Yeah.

ED. Shit, the police?

DIMITRI. OK, let's just. We have to work out what we're going to say. Let's just think properly, OK?

ED. Fuck fuck fuck.

DIMITRI. Shut the door. Guy. *(Guy goes and shuts the door.)* Put something there so —

GUY. Yeah. *(Guy wedges a chair under the door handle.)*

DIMITRI. OK. Now we think. *(A long, painful pause. They really don't know what to do. The only sound, for quite a long time, is Ed quietly sobbing.)* Anyone got a plan?

JAMES. Toby — your dad's a lawyer, right?

TOBY. No way. No fucking way. *(Chris emits a gurgling sound.)*

GUY. OK, if he's making a noise he's OK, isn't he?

MILES. Let's just go. Just walk out, they don't know who we are, we could climb out the window.

GEORGE. We can't just leave him.

DIMITRI. They've got Hugo's number, mate.

ALISTAIR. Brilliant.

DIMITRI. Should have called from the fucking landline.

MILES. Shit.

DIMITRI. If we'd fucking *talked* about it. *(Harry starts taking off his tailcoat.)*

HARRY. Take your tails off.

JAMES. Why?

HARRY. 'Cause if they know it's the club — *(Ed starts to take off his tails.)*

MILES. I don't think they'll give a shit about what we're wearing.

HARRY. If this becomes a thing, that's the club over, isn't it? If this is splashed all over every —

ALISTAIR. We say nothing, OK. Absolutely nothing.

GUY. We stick together.

JAMES. And all suffer the consequences?

GUY. We were all here, we're all, you know, involved.

DIMITRI. I don't know how far saying nothing is going to get us — the evidence pretty much speaks for itself.

ALISTAIR. Have you got a better idea?

HUGO. Self-defence. He came at us, fists all blazing, we were just defending ourselves.

DIMITRI. Ten on one?

HUGO. We were drunk and scared.

DIMITRI. Plausibility.

HARRY. We stick together, get each others' backs.

ALISTAIR. So we all say the same thing.

HUGO. We all go down together?

ED. We'll get put in prison!

JAMES. No, hang on. What about — What about we give them someone? One person. Only one person goes down.

DIMITRI. Yes — yes.

ALISTAIR. What?

JAMES. Best case scenario.

ALISTAIR. What d'you mean?

DIMITRI. I think the idea — is this right, Leighton? — is we all point the finger at one person, say it was them had the fight with the landlord.

TOBY. What, how d'you mean?

JAMES. Nine of us stay clean, only one of us goes down.

DIMITRI. If it's a one-on-one fight, it doesn't have to be a gang thing.

TOBY. What, who are we talking about?

GEORGE. What happened to looking out for each other? Isn't that what the club's for? You don't leave a man out in the field, it's not what we do.

JAMES. We'll be able to help him, yeah? One man takes a hit for the team, the rest of us pay him back later, look after him, you know, proper brotherhood.

TOBY. Who are we saying? Last in first out, or something?

HUGO. I think we should do it.

ALISTAIR. Mate, think about it.

HUGO. Not really in the market for thinking right now.

ALISTAIR. You want to get done for perjury?

HUGO. We won't get done for perjury.

ALISTAIR. What, you're a lawyer now, are you?

HUGO. I'm a chap with holes in his pockets and no one useful on speed dial is what I am. Look at me — I wouldn't last five minutes out there. I'm built for hiding in libraries. I belong at college. Not getting sent down for something I didn't fucking do. *(The boys look around at each other.)*

GUY. So which, um, which one of us? To go down.

HUGO. I think it's pretty obvious, isn't it?

TOBY. I didn't even throw the first —

DIMITRI. Ryle. You want to volunteer?

ALISTAIR. No. What?

DIMITRI. Looks quite a lot like it's your fault, mate.

HUGO. You did punch him first.

ALISTAIR. I wasn't the only person to punch him. And the rest of you wanted to, even if you didn't.

JAMES. It was you got everyone wound up.

ALISTAIR. What?

JAMES. All that stuff he said. "Fuck you, we're the Riot Club," all of that. "Stop apologising."

ALISTAIR. I only said what every other fucker in here was thinking.

ED. Incitement. It was incitement.

ALISTAIR. Oh fuck off. What, you can't think for yourself?

JAMES. I don't know how we got to a place where it's OK to do *that*. Look, from a presidential perspective I think it should be you.

ALISTAIR. You agreed — you all agreed.

JAMES. I mean this is supposed to be a dinner, right? Not a rally.

ED. Can I just say, I know I'm new here, but I think my brother would have told me if I was going to be expected to beat a man shitless.

ALISTAIR. Fucking hell.

DIMITRI. Is everyone on board?

GEORGE. I hate this.

HUGO. D'you get it, Tubes?

TOBY. Yeah. Yeah.

ALISTAIR. Fucking hell, Maitland — I went in to bat for you.

DIMITRI. When they ask you, what you going to say?

TOBY. Ryle did it.

ALISTAIR. I defended you, for Christ's sa —

DIMITRI. Anyone else?

TOBY. Just Ryle.

DIMITRI. Good man. Eddie, you're with us, yeah?

ED. Yeah yeah.

ALISTAIR. *(To Toby.)* And you punched him too — fucking booted him in the —

TOBY. Can't get a criminal record, mate.

JAMES. Sticks to you for life.

ALISTAIR. Lord Riot would be so proud.

GUY. Why can't someone sort this out?

DIMITRI. They can't, mate. But we can. Yeah?

ALISTAIR. Dimitri, you need to stop coercing people to — how fucking British d'you feel now, mate?

HUGO. Bellingfield?

DIMITRI. Mate?

GUY. OK, yeah. OK. *(To Alistair.)* Told my uncle there wouldn't even be trashing.

ALISTAIR. Milo — you hit him as well, do the honourable thing.

MILES. I want to work in America. You can't do that with a record.

ALISTAIR. That's it?

MILES. Jesus, I've only been in the club one night, I don't want to go down because of it.

GUY. I promise we'll look after you.

ALISTAIR. Villiers — mate. Come on. You know this fucking stinks.

DIMITRI. Ambulance on its way.

HARRY. If I get sent down from college —

ALISTAIR. *Mate?*

HARRY. I'm sorry.

ALISTAIR. Jesus fuck. You hit him too —

HARRY. You're the only person who's going to say that, so —

DIMITRI. George?

ALISTAIR. If you say no, mate, they can't do it. They can't do it unless they've got everyone.

JAMES. Balf, listen. We're going to be there for him, yeah? The rest of his life — next year, ten years' time, twenty. Any kind of shit hits the fan for him —

DIMITRI. The rest of us swoop in and sort it out.

ALISTAIR. Because back in the day we beat up a landlord and it made us brothers for life.

HUGO. We didn't beat up a landlord, Al. You did.

DIMITRI. Man up and take it.

ALISTAIR. We can think of something else, Balf.

DIMITRI. We haven't got time.

GEORGE. They want to save you.

ALISTAIR. They don't.

GEORGE. We're going to help him, right?

HUGO. Mate — of course.

GEORGE. Al, it's the club, isn't it?

ALISTAIR. The fucking club! You know what this is? This is — Brotherhood? Fuck off. You don't love each other, this isn't *love*, it's *fear*, you're pathetic, you're — Proud of yourselves, are you? Where's your *dignity*? Look at your faces. "How do I weasel my way out of this?" Little boys in the playground. This is the best days of your life, is it? A bear pit, a dogfight dressed up as — *(The door handle is rattled from the outside. Alistair stops.)*

RACHEL. Dad? Dad, you in there? *(The boys are still, listening. Rachel starts to bang on the door.)* Have you got my dad in there? If you don't let me in I'm calling the police. *(Alistair collects himself and opens the door. Rachel comes in, sees Chris on the floor and goes to him.)*

ALISTAIR. I'll be having a smoke. *(Alistair goes out. An ambulance siren is heard approaching. Blackout.)*

Scene 2

The gentlemen's club, as in Act One, Scene 1. Jeremy stands as Alistair comes in.

JEREMY. Alistair. How d'you do.

ALISTAIR. My lord.

JEREMY. Please! Jeremy. Title's no use when you're *modernising*. Come — sit sit. *(They sit down.)* How's your father?

ALISTAIR. Um. Alright, I think?

JEREMY. School together.

ALISTAIR. Right.

JEREMY. Glad he's put all that FSA business behind him. Rotten job, that.

ALISTAIR. It was once the *Independent* got hold of it, yes. Ten years ago now.

JEREMY. Little incident of yours won't drag it all up again, I hope.

ALISTAIR. I don't know.

JEREMY. Your father worried about that?

ALISTAIR. Among other things. Look, I've spent quite a lot of time recently getting bollocked because of this — I've disgraced my family, college, the university, and now you're going to bollock me on behalf of generations of ex-Riot Club members, frankly I've heard it all already so —

JEREMY. I haven't asked you here for a ticking off.

ALISTAIR. You haven't?

JEREMY. Drink?

ALISTAIR. Wouldn't say no. *(Jeremy pours two glasses of whisky.)*

JEREMY. Water?

ALISTAIR. Tiny slosh.

JEREMY. Ice?

ALISTAIR. Never.

JEREMY. Good man. Cheers.

ALISTAIR. Cheers. *(Jeremy drinks and sits back in his chair.)*

JEREMY. Now, it's true of course we're not entirely happy about all of this — Bingham goes to the trouble of intervening, one had assumed his *guidance* would be listened to. But the consequences for you clearly go further than a simple beasting, or whatever the weapon of choice is these days. You're due back in court when?

ALISTAIR. Next month.

JEREMY. The rotters turned you in.

ALISTAIR. Yes. Looks like it, yeah.

JEREMY. You took one for the club.

ALISTAIR. Sorry, did Guy ask you to see me?

JEREMY. Guy?

ALISTAIR. 'Cause we're not allowed to talk to each other —

JEREMY. Afraid not, no. But then that would require a reserve of courage I'm afraid my godson simply doesn't have. Whimpered like a puppy when I saw him.

ALISTAIR. He was quite sick in the night. I was in the cell next to him, I heard him crying. Hats off, though, they all kept their stories straight right through till morning.

JEREMY. When they paid their little fines and fucked off.

ALISTAIR. So if Guy didn't ask you — sorry, I'm really not sure why I'm here —

JEREMY. You're with Johnny Russell, right?

ALISTAIR. Um. Yeah.

JEREMY. Gather he's looked after your family for some years.

ALISTAIR. Since the FSA thing, yes. Dad trusts him.

JEREMY. He's a good lawyer. What's he advising, how to handle this?

ALISTAIR. I don't think I should —

JEREMY. Oh now. Come on, what's the defence line?

ALISTAIR. Russell thinks I should say I was bullied into it by the others. By the club. That they scapegoated me. Which is pretty much the truth, so —

JEREMY. So you get off and the club goes down in flames, yes?

ALISTAIR. Something like that.

JEREMY. Forgive me, would it not be better for all concerned if the club could be kept out of this?

ALISTAIR. Better for the PM?

JEREMY. I'm not acting for the PM here.

ALISTAIR. I don't see how the club could be kept out of it.

JEREMY. With the right lawyer, absolutely. Preserve your reputation *and* that of the club — see if we can't stop it getting to court entirely.

ALISTAIR. A different lawyer?

JEREMY. I know a man — ex-member himself, as it happens. Very useful at sorting out club scrapes over the years.

ALISTAIR. I think this is a bit more than a scrape.

JEREMY. You should have seen some of the others. Little incident from the '80s threatened to rear its head recently — something about a ball gag — our chap got it hushed up very effectively. I'd like to bring him in on this. Obviously, I could talk to your father for you if it's awkward or — I mean the important thing is making bloody sure that *you* come out clean.

ALISTAIR. Keeping the club clean while we're at it?

JEREMY. As I say, he'll do both.

ALISTAIR. No, then. Not interested.

JEREMY. I'm offering you —

ALISTAIR. I don't give a shit about the reputation of the club — I'm not even *in* the club, why would I want to preserve it? Smash it — what's it good for?

JEREMY. You know, I suppose, that if you go that way we'll be obliged to come after you with all the might we can muster? Paint you as an oddball, the delusional loner. People seem to understand that paradigm, don't they?

ALISTAIR. You won't have to work very hard to make them dislike me. *(Jeremy sits back in his chair.)*

JEREMY. Of course there's the other boys to think about.

ALISTAIR. All got their own lawyers, they'll be fine.

JEREMY. They're all terrified, frantically trying to second guess what you're going to do. It's a powerful position you're in. Imagine their relief if they didn't have to testify. Imagine the *gratitude*.

ALISTAIR. I don't plan on seeing them again.

JEREMY. You might find that rather difficult — unless you're planning to leave the country, you might find your lives moving along rather proximate tracks. Think about it — nine people pathetically grateful to you for the rest of your life.

ALISTAIR. I'm sorry, I know what you're doing, trying to *manage* me. I don't need managing, I know what I think. The club is fucking ridiculous. Rich little boys poncing around in tailcoats once a term? Just a bunker, isn't it? *Performing* something they haven't got the guts to be outside of the dinners. Like those fucking loons who dress up and do medieval battles. Reenactment.

JEREMY. Of course we know there's an element of silliness, letting off steam —

ALISTAIR. Training up a generation for a life in hiding. So they can end up just like you — sneaking around, desperate not to get into the papers, denying the club ever happened. Pretending you're the same as everyone else — I'm sorry, I find it shameful. Just going round in *disguise*.

JEREMY. Not disguise, no.

ALISTAIR. What then?

JEREMY. I know how you feel, I've felt it myself. The first compromise you make winds you like a rugger ball in the stomach. Stays with you like school porridge. But the next time it hurts a little less, you learn to breathe into the pain and move along and each time it's easier. Because by then you learn it's not simply disguise. It's *adaptation*.

ALISTAIR. That's just a different word for —

JEREMY. No, it's not. It's survival. We adapt to *survive*. It's what we've always done, it's what we'll continue to do. You think the country's gone to the dogs and we're going with it, but you're wrong. You can't turn a ship around on a sixpence, you know? There's a longer game to be played. My first club dinner they rolled me down a hill in a barrel full of prunes. Sick all over myself of course, laughable now, but the chap being rolled down the hill next to me, he pretty much runs the country now, and I'm not talking about the PM. What I mean is, the dinners are just the beginning. The toasts, the scrunches, the highjinks — a three-year initiation, if you like. Into something bigger, a group of people out in the world, making things happen. You might have lost your place at college and at the dinner table, but you're still in the club. You can't afford not to be. *(Jeremy takes a business card out of his pocket and holds it out to Alistair.)* I'm not just offering you a better lawyer. I'm offering you a future. One pragmatist to another — it would be worth your while to take it. *(Alistair looks at the card.)*

ALISTAIR. I need to talk to my dad, to —

JEREMY. You're an adult now. *(Alistair takes the card.)* Good.

ALISTAIR. Thank you. *(Jeremy pours another drink.)*

JEREMY. You know you're not at all what I expected. Rather thin on the ground, people like you.

ALISTAIR. What, delusional loners?

JEREMY. Independent minds. Dangerous weapon you've got there.

ALISTAIR. Can't turn it off.

JEREMY. Do you want to learn to use it to better effect?

ALISTAIR. What d'you mean?

JEREMY. Well, why don't you come and spend some time at my office, see how we do things?

ALISTAIR. I don't want anything handed to me on a plate just 'cause I —

JEREMY. I haven't offered you a constituency, Alistair. Maybe you've got it in you to do something special one day. If that's the case, I'd rather you be doing it in my camp than in someone else's. *(Jeremy's phone buzzes in his pocket and he takes it out.)* My cue to go. We'll talk again.*(Alistair puts his drink down.)* No no, please, don't get up. Stay and finish your drink, shame to waste it. Have a look around the building if you like. Not quite as fusty as it looks. *(Jeremy stands, goes to leave.)*

ALISTAIR. You loved it, didn't you? *(Jeremy is stopped in his tracks.)*

JEREMY. What?

ALISTAIR. You still love it, it's still in you. You say it's pathetic, just silly student japes. But you wouldn't have missed it for the world — the dinners, the toasting, the trashing. The Riot. *(Jeremy pauses, puts his hand on the back of his chair.)*

JEREMY. Did you know the original spelling of Lord Riot's name, wasn't R-I-O-T, but R-*Y*-O-T? Two Ts, actually.

ALISTAIR. No, I didn't.

JEREMY. Nothing to do with the idea of riotous behaviour originally. Don't know when the change happened, but there it is. Thank god someone made the switch. *(Jeremy smiles at Alistair.)*

ALISTAIR. Could have just been a mistake.

JEREMY. People like us don't make mistakes, do we? *(Jeremy leaves. Alistair settles back into his chair and looks up at the portraits on the wall. Alistair smiles. Blackout.)*

End of Play

PROPERTY LIST

2 tumblers, bottle of whisky, ice
Place settings
Vintage leather hatbox with white powdered wig
Velvet pouch with sash holding ornamental saber
Kit bag with swords
Suit carrier with tails
Packs of cigarettes, lighters
Cell phones
Burgundy leather-look menu binder
Scarf, vintage leather helmet, goggles
Motorbike keys
Icelandic bank notes
Large, scruffy rucksack
Wallet, credit card
Piece of paper
Hand-held credit card machine
Bottles of wine, wine glasses
Roll of black plastic garbage bags
Plates of foie gras
Ten-bird roast
Document
Several large wads of cash
Large dishes of Eton Mess pudding
Tray
Bottles of champagne
2 glasses, bottle of whisky

SOUND EFFECTS

Cell phone rings

NEW PLAYS

★ **MOTHERS AND SONS by Terrence McNally.** At turns funny and powerful, MOTHERS AND SONS portrays a woman who pays an unexpected visit to the New York apartment of her late son's partner, who is now married to another man and has a young son. Challenged to face how society has changed around her, generations collide as she revisits the past and begins to see the life her son might have led. "A resonant elegy for a ravaged generation." –NY Times. "A moving reflection on a changed America." –Chicago Tribune. [2M, 1W, 1 boy] ISBN: 978-0-8222-3183-7

★ **THE HEIR APPARENT by David Ives, adapted from Le Légataire Universel by Jean-François Regnard.** Paris, 1708. Eraste, a worthy though penniless young man, is in love with the fair Isabelle, but her forbidding mother, Madame Argante, will only let the two marry if Eraste can show he will inherit the estate of his rich but miserly Uncle Geronte. Unfortunately, old Geronte has also fallen for the fair Isabelle, and plans to marry her this very day and leave her everything in his will—separating the two young lovers forever. Eraste's wily servant Crispin jumps in, getting a couple of meddling relatives disinherited by impersonating them (one, a brash American, the other a French female country cousin)—only to have the old man kick off before his will is made! In a brilliant stroke, Crispin then impersonates the old man, dictating a will favorable to his master (and Crispin himself, of course)—only to find that rich Uncle Geronte isn't dead at all and is more than ever ready to marry Isabelle! The multiple strands of the plot are unraveled to great comic effect in the streaming rhyming couplets of French classical comedy, and everyone lives happily, and richly, ever after. [4M, 3W] ISBN: 978-0-8222-2808-0

★ **HANDLE WITH CARE by Jason Odell Williams.** Circumstances both hilarious and tragic bring together a young Israeli woman, who has little command of English, and a young American man, who has little command of romance. Is their inevitable love an accident…or is it destiny, generations in the making? "A hilarious and heartwarming romantic comedy." –NY Times. "Hilariously funny! Utterly charming, fearlessly adorable and a tiny bit magical." –Naples News. [2M, 2W] ISBN: 978-0-8222-3138-7

★ **LAST GAS by John Cariani.** Nat Paradis is a Red Sox-loving part-time dad who manages Paradis' Last Convenient Store, the last convenient place to get gas—or anything—before the Canadian border to the north and the North Maine Woods to the west. When an old flame returns to town, Nat gets a chance to rekindle a romance he gave up on years ago. But sparks fly as he's forced to choose between new love and old. "Peppered with poignant characters [and] sharp writing." –Portland Phoenix. "Very funny and surprisingly thought-provoking." –Portland Press Herald. [4M, 3W] ISBN: 978-0-8222-3232-2

DRAMATISTS PLAY SERVICE, INC.
440 Park Avenue South, New York, NY 10016 212-683-8960 Fax 212-213-1539
postmaster@dramatists.com www.dramatists.com

NEW PLAYS

★ **ACT ONE by James Lapine.** Growing up in an impoverished Bronx family and forced to drop out of school at age thirteen, Moss Hart dreamed of joining the glamorous world of the theater. Hart's famous memoir *Act One* plots his unlikely collaboration with the legendary playwright George S. Kaufman and his arrival on Broadway. Tony Award-winning writer and director James Lapine has adapted Act One for the stage, creating a funny, heartbreaking and suspenseful celebration of a playwright and his work. "…brims contagiously with the ineffable, irrational and irrefutable passion for that endangered religion called the Theater." –NY Times. "…wrought with abundant skill and empathy." –Time Out. [8M, 4W] ISBN: 978-0-8222-3217-9

★ **THE VEIL by Conor McPherson.** May 1822, rural Ireland. The defrocked Reverend Berkeley arrives at the crumbling former glory of Mount Prospect House to accompany a young woman to England. Seventeen-year-old Hannah is to be married off to a marquis in order to resolve the debts of her mother's estate. However, compelled by the strange voices that haunt his beautiful young charge and a fascination with the psychic current that pervades the house, Berkeley proposes a séance, the consequences of which are catastrophic. "…an effective mixture of dark comedy and suspense." –Telegraph (London). "A cracking fireside tale of haunting and decay." –Times (London). [3M, 5W] ISBN: 978-0-8222-3313-8

★ **AN OCTOROON by Branden Jacobs-Jenkins. Winner of the 2014 OBIE Award for Best New American Play.** Judge Peyton is dead and his plantation Terrebonne is in financial ruins. Peyton's handsome nephew George arrives as heir apparent and quickly falls in love with Zoe, a beautiful octoroon. But the evil overseer M'Closky has other plans—for both Terrebonne and Zoe. In 1859, a famous Irishman wrote this play about slavery in America. Now an American tries to write his own. "AN OCTOROON invites us to laugh loudly and easily at how naïve the old stereotypes now seem, until nothing seems funny at all." –NY Times [10M, 5W] ISBN: 978-0-8222-3226-1

★ **IVANOV translated and adapted by Curt Columbus.** In this fascinating early work by Anton Chekhov, we see the union of humor and pathos that would become his trademark. A restless man, Nicholai Ivanov struggles to dig himself out of debt and out of provincial boredom. When the local doctor, Lvov, informs Ivanov that his wife Anna is dying and accuses him of worsening her condition with his foul moods, Ivanov is sent into a downward spiral of depression and ennui. He soon finds himself drawn to a beautiful young woman, Sasha, full of hope and energy. Finding himself stuck between a romantic young mistress and his ailing wife, Ivanov falls deeper into crisis, heading toward inevitable tragedy. [8M, 8W] ISBN: 978-0-8222-3155-4

DRAMATISTS PLAY SERVICE, INC.
440 Park Avenue South, New York, NY 10016 212-683-8960 Fax 212-213-1539
postmaster@dramatists.com www.dramatists.com

NEW PLAYS

★ **I'LL EAT YOU LAST: A CHAT WITH SUE MENGERS by John Logan.** For more than 20 years, Sue Mengers' clients were the biggest names in show business: Barbra Streisand, Faye Dunaway, Burt Reynolds, Ali MacGraw, Gene Hackman, Cher, Candice Bergen, Ryan O'Neal, Nick Nolte, Mike Nichols, Gore Vidal, Bob Fosse…If her clients were the talk of the town, she was the town, and her dinner parties were the envy of Hollywood. Now, you're invited into her glamorous Beverly Hills home for an evening of dish, dirty secrets and all the inside showbiz details only Sue can tell you. "A delectable soufflé of a solo show…thanks to the buoyant, witty writing of Mr. Logan" –NY Times. "80 irresistible minutes of primo tinseltown dish from a certified master chef." –Hollywood Reporter. [1W] ISBN: 978-0-8222-3079-3

★ **PUNK ROCK by Simon Stephens.** In a private school outside of Manchester, England, a group of highly-articulate seventeen-year-olds flirt and posture their way through the day while preparing for their A-Level mock exams. With hormones raging and minimal adult supervision, the students must prepare for their future — and survive the savagery of high school. Inspired by playwright Simon Stephens' own experiences as a teacher, PUNK ROCK is an honest and unnerving chronicle of contemporary adolescence. "[A] tender, ferocious and frightning play." –NY Times. "[A] muscular little play that starts out funny and ferocious then reveals its compassion by degrees." –Hollywood Reporter. [5M, 3W] ISBN: 978-0-8222-3288-9

★ **THE COUNTRY HOUSE by Donald Margulies.** A brood of famous and longing-to-be-famous creative artists have gathered at their summer home during the Williamstown Theatre Festival. When the weekend takes an unexpected turn, everyone is forced to improvise, inciting a series of simmering jealousies, romantic outbursts, and passionate soul-searching. Both witty and compelling, THE COUNTRY HOUSE provides a piercing look at a family of performers coming to terms with the roles they play in each other's lives. "A valentine to the artists of the stage." –NY Times. "Remarkably candid and funny." –Variety. [3M, 3W] ISBN: 978-0-8222-3274-2

★ **OUR LADY OF KIBEHO by Katori Hall.** Based on real events, OUR LADY OF KIBEHO is an exploration of faith, doubt, and the power and consequences of both. In 1981, a village girl in Rwanda claims to see the Virgin Mary. Ostracized by her schoolmates and labeled disturbed, everyone refuses to believe, until impossible happenings appear again and again. Skepticism gives way to fear, and then to belief, causing upheaval in the school community and beyond. "Transfixing." –NY Times. "Hall's passionate play renews belief in what theater can do." –Time Out [7M, 8W, 1 boy] ISBN: 978-0-8222-3301-5

DRAMATISTS PLAY SERVICE, INC.
440 Park Avenue South, New York, NY 10016 212-683-8960 Fax 212-213-1539
postmaster@dramatists.com www.dramatists.com

NEW PLAYS

★ **AGES OF THE MOON by Sam Shepard.** Byron and Ames are old friends, reunited by mutual desperation. Over bourbon on ice, they sit, reflect and bicker until fifty years of love, friendship and rivalry are put to the test at the barrel of a gun. "A poignant and honest continuation of themes that have always been present in the work of one of this country's most important dramatists, here reconsidered in the light and shadow of time passed." –NY Times. "Finely wrought...as enjoyable and enlightening as a night spent stargazing." –Talkin' Broadway. [2M] ISBN: 978-0-8222-2462-4

★ **ALL THE WAY by Robert Schenkkan. Winner of the 2014 Tony Award for Best Play.** November, 1963. An assassin's bullet catapults Lyndon Baines Johnson into the presidency. A Shakespearean figure of towering ambition and appetite, this charismatic, conflicted Texan hurls himself into the passage of the Civil Rights Act—a tinderbox issue emblematic of a divided America—even as he campaigns for re-election in his own right, and the recognition he so desperately wants. In Pulitzer Prize and Tony Award–winning Robert Schenkkan's vivid dramatization of LBJ's first year in office, means versus ends plays out on the precipice of modern America. ALL THE WAY is a searing, enthralling exploration of the morality of power. It's not personal, it's just politics. "...action-packed, thoroughly gripping... jaw-dropping political drama." –Variety. "A theatrical coup...nonstop action. The suspense of a first-class thriller." –NY1. [17M, 3W] ISBN: 978-0-8222-3181-3

★ **CHOIR BOY by Tarell Alvin McCraney.** The Charles R. Drew Prep School for Boys is dedicated to the creation of strong, ethical black men. Pharus wants nothing more than to take his rightful place as leader of the school's legendary gospel choir. Can he find his way inside the hallowed halls of this institution if he sings in his own key? "[An] affecting and honest portrait...of a gay youth tentatively beginning to find the courage to let the truth about himself become known." –NY Times. "In his stirring and stylishly told drama, Tarell Alvin McCraney cannily explores race and sexuality and the graces and gravity of history." –NY Daily News. [7M] ISBN: 978-0-8222-3116-5

★ **THE ELECTRIC BABY by Stefanie Zadravec.** When Helen causes a car accident that kills a young man, a group of fractured souls cross paths and connect around a mysterious dying baby who glows like the moon. Folk tales and folklore weave throughout this magical story of sad endings, strange beginnings and the unlikely people that get you from one place to the next. "The imperceptible magic that pervades human existence and the power of myth to assuage sorrow are invoked by the playwright as she entwines the lives of strangers in THE ELECTRIC BABY, a touching drama." –NY Times. "As dazzling as the dialogue is dreamful." –Pittsburgh City Paper. [3M, 3W] ISBN: 978-0-8222-3011-3

DRAMATISTS PLAY SERVICE, INC.
440 Park Avenue South, New York, NY 10016 212-683-8960 Fax 212-213-1539
postmaster@dramatists.com www.dramatists.com